# THE SPACE SHUTTLE *CHALLENGER* DISASTER IN AMERICAN HISTORY

# The IN AMERICAN HISTORY Series

# THE SPACE SHUTTLE *CHALLENGER* DISASTER IN AMERICAN HISTORY

Suzanne Lieurance

**Enslow Publishers, Inc.**

40 Industrial Road        PO Box 38
Box 398                   Aldershot
Berkeley Heights, NJ 07922    Hants GU12 6BP
USA                               UK

http://www.enslow.com

*To my husband, Adrian Lieurance, for all his love, help, and support. And to Miko, my little four-footed writing buddy.*

**Library of Congress Cataloging-in-Publication Data**

Lieurance, Suzanne.
    The space shuttle Challenger disaster in American history / Suzanne Lieurance.
        p. cm. — (In American history)
    Includes bibliographical references (p. ) and index.
    ISBN 0-7660-1419-3
    1. Challenger (Spacecraft)—Juvenile literature. 2. Challenger (Spacecraft)—Accidents—Juvenile literature. 3. McAuliffe, Christa, 1948–1986—Juvenile literature. 4. Teachers—United States—Juvenile literature. 5. Manned space flight—Juvenile literature. [1. Challenger (Spacecraft)—Accidents. 2. Space shuttles—Accidents] I. Title. II. Series.
    TL795.515 .L54   2001
    363.12'465—dc21
                                    00-009711

Printed in the United States of America

10 9 8 7 6 5 4 3 2 1

**To Our Readers:** All Internet Addresses in this book were active and appropriate at the time we went to press. Any comments or suggestions can be sent by e-mail to Comments@enslow.com or to the address on the back cover.

**Illustration Credits:** Enslow Publishers, Inc., p. 77; National Aeronautics and Space Administration, pp. 18, 25, 30, 32, 36, 50, 52, 55, 57, 59, 60, 63, 64, 81, 84, 92, 95, 99, 102, 106, 118; NASA/LBJ Space Center, pp. 11, 13, 24, 28, 43, 65, 70, 85.

**Cover Illustration:** National Aeronautics and Space Administration.

# ★ CONTENTS ★

Tuesday, January 28, 1986, was a clear and unusually cold day at Cape Canaveral, Florida. But it was an exciting day. The space shuttle *Challenger* sat on the launchpad. For the first time ever, a schoolteacher would be part of the crew. Sharon Christa McAuliffe, from Concord,

# LIFTOFF TO DISASTER

New Hampshire, had been selected by the National Aeronautics and Space Administration (NASA) to be the first teacher in space. She was scheduled to do experiments and teach two lessons that would be sent back to students on Earth.

This shuttle mission would have other special purposes as well. Astronauts would launch a satellite that would carry out scientific experiments and collect information about Halley's comet. Experiments would also be performed aboard the shuttle flight to study how fluids act in orbit.

Now the world waited to see if this would finally be the day *Challenger* flight 51-L launched.

## The World Waits

On Monday, January 27, the world had waited. The seven *Challenger* crew members had waited, too. Lying flat on their backs, strapped to their seats, they waited for several hours. The launch was eventually postponed because the winds were gusting up to thirty miles an hour—too strong for the shuttle to attempt a landing if an emergency developed. "It was just not our day," said Robert Seick, the director of shuttle operations.[1]

By Monday evening, things were not looking much better. A record cold front was due, with subfreezing temperatures and arctic wind-chill factors. A shuttle had never been launched at a temperature below 53°F. Would *Challenger* be the first? The evening news reports were not hopeful.

As the next day, Tuesday, January 28, dawned, the *Challenger* crew heard about the weather. They worried that the flight might be canceled again. Although they hoped it would not be canceled, it was actually too cold for a safe launch. Engineers were concerned that cold temperatures could cause the O-rings—the rubber seals between the rocket's segments—to weaken and allow explosive gases to leak. But this concern never reached the proper NASA officials.

## Flight 51-L

Each shuttle flight is given a specific mission number. *Challenger* flight 51-L was so named for several reasons. The number "5" indicated that the flight was scheduled for 1985. The number "1" meant the flight would launch from Kennedy Space Center. The letter "L" meant that this would be the twelfth flight of the

ON FLIGHT DAY 1, AFTER ARRIVING INTO ORBIT, THE CREW WAS TO HAVE TWO PERIODS OF SCHEDULED HIGH ACTIVITY. FIRST THEY WERE TO CHECK THE READINESS OF THE *TDRS-B* SATELLITE PRIOR TO PLANNED DEPLOYMENT. AFTER LUNCH THEY WERE TO DEPLOY THE SATELLITE AND ITS *INERTIAL UPPER STAGE* (IUS) BOOSTER AND TO PERFORM A SERIES OF SEPARATION MANEUVERS. THE FIRST SLEEP PERIOD WAS SCHEDULED TO BE EIGHT HOURS LONG STARTING ABOUT 18 HOURS AFTER CREW WAKEUP THE MORNING OF LAUNCH.

ON FLIGHT DAY 2, THE COMET HALLEY ACTIVE MONITORING PROGRAM *(CHAMP)* EXPERIMENT WAS SCHEDULED TO BEGIN. ALSO SCHEDULED WERE THE INITIAL "TEACHER IN SPACE" . . . VIDEO TAPING AND A FIRING OF THE ORBITAL MANEUVERING ENGINES *(OMS)* TO PLACE *CHALLENGER* AT THE 152-MILE ORBITAL ALTITUDE FROM WHICH THE SPARTAN WOULD BE DEPLOYED.

ON FLIGHT DAY 3, THE CREW WAS TO BEGIN PRE-DEPLOYMENT PREPARATIONS ON THE *SPARTAN* AND THEN THE SATELLITE WAS TO BE DEPLOYED USING THE REMOTE MANIPULATOR SYSTEM *(RMS)* ROBOT ARM. THEN THE FLIGHT CREW WAS TO SLOWLY SEPARATE FROM *SPARTAN* BY 90 MILES.

ON FLIGHT DAY 4, THE *CHALLENGER* WAS TO BEGIN CLOSING ON *SPARTAN* WHILE GREGORY B. JARVIS CONTINUED FLUID DYNAMICS EXPERIMENTS STARTED ON DAY TWO AND DAY 3. LIVE TELECASTS WERE ALSO PLANNED TO BE CONDUCTED BY CHRISTA MCAULIFFE.

ON FLIGHT DAY 5, THE CREW WAS TO RENDEZVOUS WITH *SPARTAN* AND USE THE ROBOT ARM TO CAPTURE THE SATELLITE AND RE-STOW IT IN THE PAYLOAD BAY.

ON FLIGHT DAY 6, RE-ENTRY PREPARATIONS WERE SCHEDULED. THIS INCLUDED FLIGHT CONTROL CHECKS, TEST FIRING OF MANEUVERING JETS NEEDED FOR REENTRY, AND CABIN STOWAGE. A CREW NEWS CONFERENCE WAS ALSO SCHEDULED FOLLOWING THE LUNCH PERIOD.

ON FLIGHT DAY 7, THE DAY WOULD HAVE BEEN SPENT PREPARING THE SPACE SHUTTLE FOR *DEORBIT* AND ENTRY INTO THE ATMOSPHERE. THE *CHALLENGER* WAS SCHEDULED TO LAND AT THE *KENNEDY SPACE CENTER* 144 HOURS AND 34 MINUTES AFTER LAUNCH.[2]

*Prior to the* Challenger *disaster, NASA had outlined the objectives the crew was supposed to accomplish.*

year, since *L* is the twelfth letter of the alphabet. As the number "5" indicated, flight 51-L was originally supposed to take place in July 1985. By the time the crew was assigned in January 1985, the launch had been postponed to November. The launch was later delayed further until it was finally rescheduled for late January 1986. NASA had a tight shuttle schedule for 1986. If flight 51-L were delayed any longer, it would delay the flights that were scheduled to follow it.

Now, unaware that cold weather could create dangerous problems, NASA officials decided that the time had come to launch. The world had already waited too long.

## The Waiting Ends

At 7:30 A.M. on Tuesday, the crew received a final weather briefing. They were hopeful about the launch. No one explained to them the dangers of launching on such a cold day. Even the experienced astronauts did not realize how great a hazard such cold temperatures could be. No one told Commander Francis "Dick" Scobee that the O-ring seals might not function in cold weather. As the commander of the mission, he had the authority to decide whether they would launch that day. But he did not have the full information, so he was excited about the launch. "My kind of weather," he said. "What a great day for flying!"[3]

A few minutes later, Commander Scobee led his crew down a cement ramp, past a crowd of journalists, to a van that would take them to the launchpad.

Photographers shouted McAuliffe's name.

"We're going to go off today!" McAuliffe said, as she waved good-bye.[4]

At the launchpad, Scobee was the first to enter the orbiter. He was followed by crew members Mike Smith and Judith Resnik.

As McAuliffe approached the hatch, Johnny Corlew, an inspector, had a gift for her. It was a red apple, just like the ones he used to pick for his teachers from his family's apple tree back home. Now, he surely did not want to miss the chance to give an apple to America's Teacher in Space. He offered it to McAuliffe, who smiled and handed it back to him.

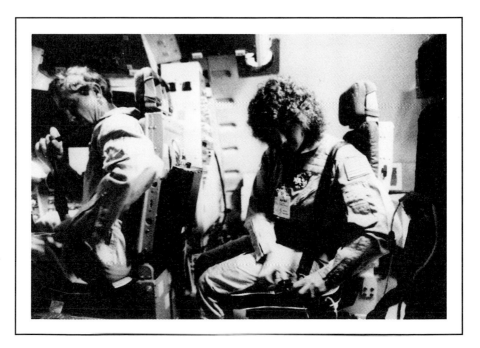

*Christa McAuliffe and the crew prepare for liftoff.*

"Save it for me," she said, "and I'll eat it when I get back."[5] McAuliffe would never get to eat that apple, however. She would not be coming back. Commander Dick Scobee; pilot Mike Smith; mission specialists Judith Resnik, Ron McNair, and Ellison Onizuka; and payload specialist Gregory Jarvis would not be coming back, either. This time, NASA should have waited, but did not.

## Disaster

Excited friends, relatives, teachers, schoolchildren, and dignitaries had gathered at the viewing stands to watch the launch. McAuliffe's family, including her husband, two children, and both of her parents, waited anxiously. Commander Scobee's grown daughter, twenty-five-year-old Kathie, huddled in the cold with her mother, brother, and infant son to watch the launch with other families of the *Challenger* crew who were assembled on the roof of the launch control center. Everyone joined in the countdown.

Five . . . four . . . three . . . two . . . one . . . Liftoff!

The crowd cheered as *Challenger* left the launchpad at exactly 11:38 A.M.

McAuliffe's students in New Hampshire watched on television monitors at their school. Students and teachers in classrooms across the country watched, too. Everywhere, time seemed to stand still as viewers sat in front of their television sets or looked up to the sky.

Over the loudspeaker at Cape Canaveral came the voices of the *Challenger* crew and Mission Control.

"*Challenger* now heading downrange," said Mission Control, "engines beginning to throttle down to 94 percent. . . . Will throttle down to 65 percent shortly. Velocity, 2,257 feet per second. Altitude 4.3 nautical miles. Three engines running normally. . . . Engines throttling up. Three engines now at 104 percent!"

"Go, you mother!" said pilot Mike Smith. "There's 10,000 feet and Mach point five." *Challenger* was now traveling at half the speed of sound.

"Point nine," said Commander Scobee.

"There's Mach One," said Smith. *Challenger* was now traveling faster than the speed of sound. It continued to climb.

*Flight directors Jay H. Greene (rear) and Alan L. Briscoe (foreground) at Mission Control on January 28, the morning of the* Challenger *liftoff.*

**CDR**: SCOBEE
**PLT**: SMITH
**MS 1**: ONIZUKA
**MS 2**: RESNIK

**T+**: INDICATES TIME (SECONDS AFTER LIFTOFF)

**T+11 PLT**: GO YOU MOTHER.
**T+14 MS**: LVLH. . . .
(NASA: REMINDER FOR COCKPIT SWITCH CONFIGURATION CHANGE.)
**T+15 MS 2**: (EXPLETIVE) HOT.
**T+16 CDR**: OOOHH-KAAAY.
**T+19 PLT**: LOOKS LIKE WE'VE GOT A LOTTA WIND HERE TODAY.
**T+20 CDR**: YEAH.
**T+22 CDR**: IT'S A LITTLE HARD TO SEE OUT MY WINDOW HERE.
**T+28 PLT**: THERE'S TEN THOUSAND FEET AND MACH POINT FIVE. . . .
**T+40 PLT**: THERE'S MACH ONE.
(NASA: VELOCITY REPORT, 1.0 MACH.)
**T+41 CDR**: GOING THROUGH NINETEEN THOUSAND.
(NASA: ALTITUDE REPORT, 19,000 FT.)
**T+43 CDR**: OK WE'RE THROTTLING DOWN.
(NASA: NORMAL SSME THRUST REDUCTION DURING MAXIMUM DYNAMIC PRESSURE REGION.)
**T+57 CDR**: THROTTLING UP.
(NASA: THROTTLE UP TO 104% AFTER MAXIMUM DYNAMIC PRESSURE.)
**T+58 PLT**: THROTTLE UP.
**T+59 CDR**: ROGER.
**T+60 PLT**: FEEL THAT MOTHER GO.
**T+60** WOOOOHOOOO.
**T+1:02 PLT**: THIRTY-FIVE THOUSAND GOING THROUGH ONE POINT FIVE
(NASA: ALTITUDE AND VELOCITY REPORT, 35,000 FT., 1.5 MACH.)
**T+1:05 CDR**: READING FOUR EIGHTY SIX ON MINE.
(NASA: ROUTINE AIRSPEED INDICATOR CHECK.)
**T+1:07 PLT**: YEP, THAT'S WHAT I'VE GOT, TOO.
**T+1:10 CDR**: ROGER, GO AT THROTTLE UP.
(NASA: SSME AT 104 PERCENT.)
**T+1:13 PLT**: UHOH.
**T+1:13** LOSS OF ALL DATA.[7]

*During the investigation of the explosion, NASA studied the transcripts of the last recorded words of the crew members.*

"Thirty-five thousand. Going through 1.5," Smith said.

"*Challenger*, go at throttle up," said Mission Control.[6]

Then, without warning, seventy-three seconds after *Challenger* left the launchpad, the unthinkable happened. A cloud of white smoke and orange fire filled the sky. The shuttle had exploded.

"They're gone," said Jane Smith, wife of pilot Michael Smith.

"What do you mean, Mom?" asked her son, Scott.

"They're lost," she replied.[8]

Cheers from the crowd turned to silence. People were stunned. They could not believe what they had just witnessed.

Families of the crew were whisked off the roof and from the VIP bleachers. They were led into elevators and put into buses.

The last recorded words from any of *Challenger*'s crew were those of pilot Mike Smith.

"Uh oh," he said.[9]

# 2

## THE BEGINNING OF THE SPACE PROGRAM

Life was very different back in the late 1950s when Christa McAuliffe and other members of the *Challenger* crew were still children or in their teens. A little more than a decade had passed since the end of World War II. Dwight David Eisenhower was the president. *Ozzie and Harriet*—a TV program about the life of an everyday American family—was popular. Many things that modern Americans take for granted today, such as personal computers and VCRs, had not been invented yet. Even the space program was just beginning. People in the United States huddled around black-and-white television sets to keep up with the latest world developments.

### A Race Begins

Sharon Christa McAuliffe was just nine years old in 1957. It was that year when this alarming message about startling scientific developments in the Soviet Union's space program came across the Associated Press machines in newsrooms throughout the United States:

LONDON. OCT. 4 (AP)—MOSCOW RADIO SAID
TONIGHT THAT THE SOVIET UNION HAS LAUNCHED AN
EARTH SATELLITE. THE SATELLITE, SILVER IN COLOR,
WEIGHS 184 POUNDS AND IS REPORTED TO BE THE SIZE
OF A BASKETBALL. MOSCOW RADIO SAID IT IS CIRCLING
THE GLOBE EVERY 96 MINUTES, REACHING AS FAR OUT
AS 569 MILES AS IT ZIPS ALONG AT MORE THAN 17,000
MILES PER HOUR.[1]

Soon the news was on every radio and television
station across the country. It made headlines in newspapers everywhere. Young Christa did not pay much
attention to all the fuss, but people around the world
were in a state of shock—especially the adults of the
United States. Until now they had thought their country would be the first in space. This bulletin proved
otherwise.

The Soviets had successfully launched a satellite.
The satellite, called *Sputnik*, was twenty-three inches in
diameter, about twice the size of a basketball, but it
could be heard with radio receivers around the world.
*Life* magazine reported that its beeping "sounded like
a cricket with a cold."[2]

Everyone who heard this beeping understood what
it meant. A space race between the two strongest
world powers—the United States and the Soviet
Union—had officially begun. But it was not just a
space race. It was an arms race, too. Rockets used to
launch satellites were modified missiles. With the
launching of *Sputnik*, the Soviet Union was making a
display of power that left the United States no choice
but to keep up. If the Soviets were able to send missiles

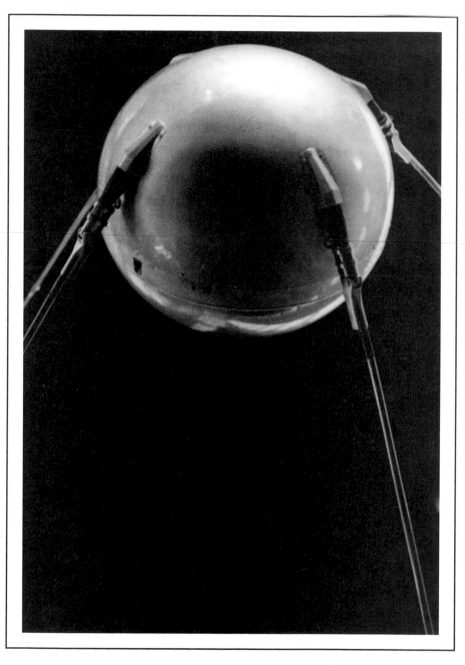

*In 1957, when the Soviet Union launched* Sputnik, *the United States became determined to win the space race.*

to the United States, then Americans wanted to show that they could protect themselves by sending missiles to the Soviet Union, too.

Actually, the United States had been working on a satellite for a long time. In fact, while the Soviets were busy developing *Sputnik*, two separate groups of scientists in the United States were studying rockets and satellites. One group consisted of 118 German scientists who were recruited by the United States after Germany's defeat in World War II. These scientists were members of the most prized rocket team of Adolf Hitler's Nazi government. After the war, they were hired to design, construct, test, and launch long-range missiles for the United States. They had been recruited through something called Operation Paperclip—a secret United States Army program that searched all over Germany for rocket, atomic, and aircraft specialists who could be brought to America as a team.

The lead German scientist was a man named Dr. Wernher von Braun. Von Braun was a brilliant engineer who, when he was a boy, had dreamed of developing rockets to explore outer space. When World War II started, he and many other engineers had been forced to build destructive weapons for Adolf Hitler. When the war ended and Germany was defeated, von Braun knew that he and his colleagues did not want to fall into the hands of the Soviets, who were still angry about the German invasion. Surrendering to the Americans was much safer than letting the Soviets capture them, so von Braun and his colleagues decided to work for the United States.

At that time, the United States did not have a rocket program. The country did not quite know what to do with von Braun and his team. They were first sent to Fort Bliss, Texas, to teach rocketry to interested army personnel. In 1950, when the army learned that the Soviets were moving ahead with rocket research, the United States decided to establish its own rocket research and development center.

Von Braun and his team were sent to Huntsville, Alabama, to design rockets. Huntsville was the location of the army's Redstone Arsenal, which was no longer used. Government officials felt it would make a perfect site for a new rocket program. Unfortunately for von Braun, Americans were still recovering from the effects of World War II. They were not very hospitable to him and his crew of German scientists. They suspected him of being a Nazi. Gradually, they were won over by von Braun's outgoing personality and hard work. They began to respect and support him and his fellow scientists.

Still, there were reports that President Eisenhower and his aides wanted the world's first satellite to be orbited by an American scientific team, not by von Braun and his crew. This second group of American scientists became known as the Vanguard team, named for the *Vanguard* rocket they were trying to develop.

Before the successful launch of *Sputnik*, the United States had been considered the world's unchallenged leader in technology, with the Soviets trailing far behind. Now the Soviet Union had shown the world that this was not true. The Soviet Union was just as advanced as the United States.

A Soviet satellite posed a threat to United States national security. Never before had other nations been able to launch a rocket into United States airspace. President Eisenhower tried to make light of the situation and minimize the threat it represented. "After all," he said at a news conference, "the Russians have only put one small ball in the air."[3]

Premier Nikita Khrushchev, the leader of the Soviet government, saw the development of *Sputnik* as much more than that. "People of the whole world are pointing to the satellite," he boasted. "They are saying the U.S. has been beaten."[4]

But things were not exactly as they appeared. According to documents later published, the United States had planned for the Soviet Union to win this first round of the space race.[5] The Eisenhower administration wanted the Soviet Union to be the first to fly over United States airspace, rather than the United States being first to fly over Soviet airspace. It had never before been established that national boundaries do not stretch infinitely upward into space. By allowing the Soviets to violate another country's airspace first, the United States would not face diplomatic or legal complications from other countries when it launched its own satellites.

## The Soviets Take Another Step

Thirty days after the launch of *Sputnik*, the Soviets took another, even more astonishing, step in the space race. They launched *Sputnik 2*. It weighed an amazing 1,120 pounds and soared as high as 1,031 miles. America had been struggling with its own three-pound satellite.

Now the Soviets had put a second satellite into orbit. Not only was it huge, but it also contained a living, breathing creature—a dog named Laika. The heartbeat of a live animal being transmitted back to Earth was much more impressive than any mechanical beeping could ever be. Surely this meant it would not be long before the Soviets sent a human being into space. If the United States did not keep up, the Soviets would win the space race by being the first to put a man on the moon. The United States could not let that happen.

## The Next Step

The United States was becoming very anxious. President Eisenhower wanted American scientists to launch a satellite and show the world that the United States could keep up with the Soviet Union. Under pressure from Eisenhower's administration, the Vanguard team rushed its rocket to a launchpad at Cape Canaveral, in Florida. The press gathered to witness the event. But, on December 6, 1957, the day of the scheduled launch, as it tried to take off, the *Vanguard* caught fire, broke apart, and exploded. The tiny satellite rolled into the bushes. This was humiliating for the United States. Something had to be done.

President Eisenhower gave von Braun and his team permission to launch their satellite. On January 31, 1958, a rocket was launched, and the satellite, named *Explorer 1*, went into orbit around the earth. Von Braun became a hero. He had enabled the United States to take its first step in the space race, even though Americans were still trailing behind the Soviets.

Several months later, in July 1958, President Eisenhower formed the National Aeronautics and Space Administration (NASA). Today, it is the agency that operates all United States space programs. The space race was getting serious.

## More Steps

On April 12, 1961, the Soviets moved even farther ahead in the race. Soviet cosmonaut (astronaut) Yuri Gagarin became the first human to go into space. "I saw for the first time," he said, "the earth's shape. I could easily see the shores of continents, islands, great rivers, folds of the terrain, large bodies of water. The horizon is dark blue, smoothly turning to black. . . . the feelings which filled me I can express with one word—joy."[6]

Gagarin completed one orbit of Earth, lasting one hour and forty-eight minutes. Though it seemed the United States would never catch up with the Soviets, just three weeks later, Alan B. Shepard, Jr., became the

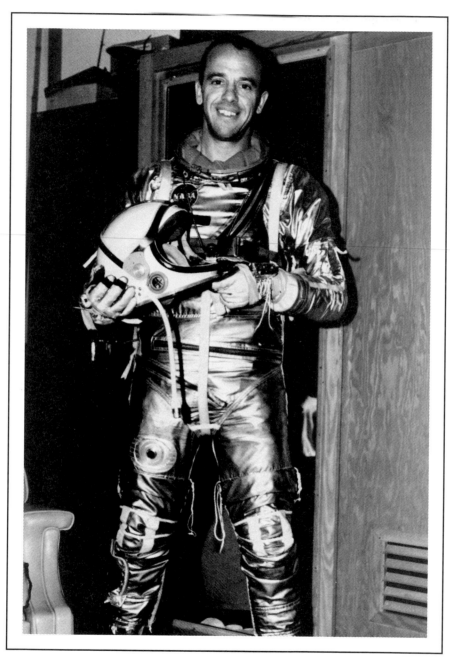

*Alan Shepard, Jr., was the first American to take a space flight, in 1961.*

first American in space. His flight lasted a total of only fifteen minutes twenty-two seconds, and he did not go into orbit. However, on February 20, 1962, John Glenn, Jr., became the first American to do so. He circled Earth three times in four hours and fifty-five minutes.

The next year, Valentina Tereshkova, a Soviet cosmonaut, became the first woman in space. In 1965, Alexei Leonov, another Soviet, became the first person to walk in space. Tethered to his spacecraft, he walked

*John H. Glenn, Jr., completed the first American orbital flight in the* Friendship 7 *spacecraft.*

outside it. About this time, the Americans began the Gemini project. It sent ten missions into space.

After President Eisenhower left office in 1961, President John F. Kennedy did all he could to promote space exploration. He raised educational standards and funded organizations that researched and studied space in hopes of reaching the moon first. In a 1961 speech to Congress, Kennedy declared that the nation's goal would be, by 1970, to land a man on the moon and return him safely to Earth. He said,

> This decision demands a major national commitment of scientific and technical manpower, material and facilities . . . it means a degree of dedication, organization, and discipline which have not always characterized our research and development effort.
>
> Every scientist, every engineer, every serviceman, every technician, contractor, and civil servant involved gives his personal pledge that this nation will move forward, with the full speed of freedom, in the exciting adventure of space.[7]

But even with the "full speed of freedom," sending a man to the moon could not be done quickly. It took many steps. Both Kennedy and Lyndon Johnson, who became president in 1963 after Kennedy was assassinated, poured millions of dollars into the space program. In the late 1960s, the Gemini project led to a series of Apollo missions.

*Apollo 1* was scheduled for liftoff on February 1, 1967. It was to be the first piloted Apollo mission into space. But the spacecraft never left the ground. On January 27, during training, three astronauts—Virgil

Grissom, Edward White II, and Roger Chaffee—were in the command module when disaster struck. An electrical fire started and spread quickly. All three astronauts died. This was the worst space-related disaster the United States had yet seen. Still, it did not stop Americans from continuing the race. They could not afford to give up.

There were many more Apollo missions. Each one taught NASA and American astronauts something new about space travel that would bring the United States one step closer to its goal of landing a human being on the moon.

## Crossing the Finish Line

On July 20, 1969, the landing module (a small space vehicle called the *Eagle*) of *Apollo 11* reached the moon with astronauts Neil Armstrong and Buzz Aldrin, Jr., inside it. While Armstrong and Aldrin were making history on the moon's surface, astronaut Michael Collins stayed in the command module, orbiting the moon. When Armstrong stepped on the surface of the moon, he declared, "That's one small step for man . . . one giant leap for mankind."[8] People everywhere knew the United States had crossed the finish line and won the space race.

Richard M. Nixon, who was then president of the United States, spoke by radio to these three astronauts so far away. "Because of what you have done, the heavens have become part of man's world," he told them. "As you talk to us from the Sea of Tranquility, it

*These men made up the first American space team. Virgil Grissom (back row, center) was killed in the Apollo 1 spacecraft disaster in 1967.*

inspires us to redouble our efforts to bring peace and tranquility to man. All the people on Earth are surely one in their pride for what you have done."[9]

After the United States became the first nation to land on the moon, many Americans lost interest in the space program. There were many other Apollo flights, but none as dramatic and exciting as *Apollo 11*.

## Space Stations Are Established

After the Apollo missions, the next big goal in space exploration was to establish a permanent space station where people could live for long periods of time. The United States and the Soviet Union each launched experimental space stations in the 1970s. These stations stayed in orbit, and teams of astronauts went back and forth to them in rockets, setting records for time spent in space.

## The Space Shuttle Is Born

As the 1970s began, the United States was faced with many other concerns besides space travel. Attention turned to the war in Vietnam, civil rights issues, and an energy crisis. The space program was enormously expensive. Many Americans felt money could be better spent on other things.

It cost hundreds of millions of dollars each time a rocket was launched into space, and each rocket could be used only once. As a result, the space program had few strong supporters in Congress, and NASA's budget was drastically cut. Scientists began to make plans

*The United States made great strides in the space race by successfully landing American astronauts on the moon in July 1969.*

for a reusable space vehicle—a space shuttle. Congress liked this idea because it would save money.

At first, the space shuttle was envisioned as a fully reusable, commercial spaceplane. However, its development faced considerable problems. Among these were budget cuts (when projected costs for the shuttle kept increasing), design difficulties, and a lack of interest from the public. As a result, scientists eventually developed a smaller, semi-reusable vehicle known as the space shuttle.

The first shuttle ever built was never launched out of the atmosphere. Named the *Enterprise*, it was first used for manned test flights. Eventually, it was kept for spare parts for the rest of the shuttle fleet. The other three shuttles in the fleet were *Columbia*, *Atlantis*, and *Challenger*.

*Columbia*, the first shuttle to launch, lifted off from Pad A on Launch Complex 39, Kennedy Space Center, on April 12, 1981. After a two-day test-flight mission that verified *Columbia*'s ability to function in space, it landed at Edwards Air Force Base in California. The vehicle was piloted by John Young and Robert Crippen. The mission marked the first time that a new space vehicle carried a crew on its initial flight.

Over the next few years, space shuttles took off frequently. In June 1983, Sally Ride became the first American woman in space aboard the space shuttle *Challenger*.

*Sally Ride, the first American woman in space, took her historic flight in the space shuttle* Challenger.

After twenty-four successful flights of the space shuttle, it was not "news" anymore. Shuttle launches became routine.

Republican President Ronald Reagan was running for re-election in 1984. His opponent was Democrat Walter Mondale. Mondale was formally endorsed by the National Education Association as its choice for president on July 4. Later that year, a Gallup Poll showed that a large majority of Americans believed Walter Mondale would be more likely than President Reagan to improve public education. It was clear that President Reagan had to do something to show the public that this belief was wrong.

On Friday, August 27, 1984, Reagan made an announcement. "Until now," he said,

> we hadn't decided who the first citizen passenger [in space] would be. But today I'm directing NASA to begin a search in all our elementary and secondary schools and to choose as the first citizen passenger in our space program, one of America's finest, a teacher.[10]

It would take NASA months to select the perfect teacher for this mission. The search was on.

# 3

# THE SEARCH FOR A TEACHER IN SPACE

Schoolteacher Christa McAuliffe heard President Reagan's announcement that a teacher would soon be a passenger on the space shuttle. She was excited. She knew she wanted to apply.

Called Christa from an early age, Sharon Christa Corrigan was born on September 2, 1948, in Boston, Massachusetts, the eldest of five children. Christa's family later moved to Framingham, Massachusetts. Christa attended Marian High, a coeducational Catholic high school. It was there that she met and dated Steven McAuliffe, who would later become her husband.

After high school graduation in 1966, Christa went to college at nearby Framingham State College. She majored in history and received her degree in 1970. Soon after graduation, she and Steve were married. They moved to Washington, D.C., where Steve attended law school. Christa became a junior high school teacher. She was also a student herself, studying for a master's degree in school administration at Bowie State College in Maryland.

In 1976, the McAuliffes' first child was born, a son named Scott Corrigan McAuliffe. In 1979, daughter Caroline was born. By that time, the McAuliffes had moved to Concord, New Hampshire. At first, Christa McAuliffe did not return to teaching. She stayed home to care for her children. But soon, she was back in the classroom.

McAuliffe always had an adventurous spirit. Becoming the first teacher in space would be a unique opportunity. She became determined to give it a shot.

## The Teacher in Space Program Begins

In November 1984, NASA distributed something called an "Announcement of Opportunity." It was like a job advertisement. It described how the teacher in space would be chosen. It listed the medical requirements for candidates and explained what would be expected of the teacher who was selected.

Teachers from the United States and its territories could apply from December 1, 1984, to February 1, 1985. Though applicants only had to have five years' teaching experience, the application itself was very extensive. It had twenty-five pages of instructions, essay questions, requests for background information, and recommendations. Only those who were seriously interested would go to all the trouble of filling it out. Christa McAuliffe was one of them. "Go for it," said her husband, Steve.[1]

NASA used this logo for its Teacher in Space program.

She did, along with eleven thousand other teachers. Applications came in from teachers from all fifty states, the District of Columbia, Puerto Rico, Guam, the Virgin Islands, overseas United States schools, and Bureau of Indian Affairs schools (schools on Indian reservations).

One of the application questions asked why the applicant wanted to travel in space. McAuliffe answered,

> I remember when Alan Shepard made his historic flight—not even in orbit—and I was thrilled. I cannot join the space program and restart my life as an astronaut, but this . . . is an opportunity to fulfill my early fantasies. I watched the Space Age being born, and I would like to participate.[2]

McAuliffe practiced answering interview questions by taping herself with a video camera. One of the things NASA wanted to know was how being part of the program would change her life.

"It will change my life—I think it will give me an opportunity to meet a lot of people and to share the space age, which right now is kind of removed," she said into the camera.[3]

NASA also wanted to know about her philosophy of life. She said her philosophy was to get as much as possible out of life.

Months went by. McAuliffe heard nothing from NASA.

Review panels were going through all the applications, selecting two semifinalists from each state and

United States territory. This process narrowed the number of teachers to 114 candidates.

Finally, news came in April 1985. McAuliffe was among the 114 candidates.

The list of candidates was impressive. Some were doctors and authors, as well as teachers. McAuliffe was none of these. She was simply an excellent teacher and an ordinary person who wanted to do something extraordinary.

"I'm out of my league. I haven't got a chance!" she told her husband, after reading the biographies of some of the other candidates.[4]

## The Search Narrows

On June 22, 1985, McAuliffe traveled to Washington, D.C., with the 113 other nominees. During their seven-day stay, a national review panel of distinguished people would select ten finalists for the competition. The panel was made up of a diverse group of people— three former astronauts, a former United States commissioner of education, three college presidents and administrators, a former state governor, a former United States congressman, four educators, a former NASA official, a former professional basketball player, two business executives, two professional actors, and a physicist.

McAuliffe was asked what special project she would suggest if she were chosen for the program. She said she wanted to keep a journal, just as the early American pioneers had done when they traveled west.

McAuliffe had been keeping a journal herself for years. She also required her students to keep a daily journal as part of their work for a special course called "The American Woman" that she created and taught back at her high school in Concord. Through developing this course she learned that much information about the social history of the United States has been found in the diaries of common people. "So like a woman on the Conestoga wagons pioneering the West, I too would be able to bring back my thoughts in my journal, to make that a part of history."[5]

She went on to explain that her journal would be a trilogy (three parts). The first part would begin at the point of selection and include the training for the program. The second part would cover the flight itself. The third part would cover her thoughts, reflections, and experiences after her return from the voyage.

Most of the other candidates were proposing more complicated projects to develop if they were selected for the program. In contrast, a journal must have sounded very simple, but the judges were impressed. McAuliffe was now a finalist!

## The Finalists Go to Texas

On July 7, 1985, the ten finalists went to Johnson Space Center in Houston, Texas. Here they would be tested and interviewed further by the NASA Space Flight Participant Evaluation Committee. Then, over the next several days, they would undergo complete medical examinations, physical and psychological fitness tests, and briefings about space flight.

One test involved an altitude test chamber. This special chamber simulates sudden drastic changes in altitude, like those that astronauts experience in space. The finalists would have to learn to recognize the symptoms of a lack of oxygen within their bodies. As soon as symptoms appeared, they had to get oxygen immediately. McAuliffe recognized the symptoms. As soon as she had difficulty breathing and her vision became blurry, she reached for her oxygen mask.

Another test involved riding in a KC-135. This airplane, nicknamed the "vomit comet," is like riding a roller coaster in the sky. It goes up "hills" of ten thousand feet and then drops, so that people inside are weightless for about twenty-five seconds. Then they experience about twice the force of gravity. Many people, including astronauts, become sick to their stomachs during these flights. McAuliffe was a bit concerned about the KC-135. As a child she could not go on amusement park rides without throwing up. She wondered how she could make it on this "vomit comet."

The KC-135 flew McAuliffe and the other teachers in roller-coaster-like loops, over and over again. For a few moments during each loop, the teachers floated in the air, experiencing weightlessness, much as they would if they were traveling in space. McAuliffe bounced around from wall to wall of the aircraft. Her hair stood on end—but she did not throw up. She passed the test.

Sometimes astronauts must be confined to small, enclosed spaces. To find out if any of the teachers were fearful of being in an enclosed space, McAuliffe and the other candidates had to spend ten minutes curled up inside a fabric ball, called a personal rescue sphere (nicknamed PRS by NASA employees). The PRS was an inflatable nylon ball only thirty-four inches in diameter, linked to an oxygen supply and zipped shut from the outside. The ball was being developed for emergencies. Since only two space suits fit on board the shuttle, in case of emergency, two of the astronauts (probably the commander and the pilot) would slip into these space suits, zip the rest of the crew into personal rescue spheres, and carry them weightlessly to another shuttle or an orbiting space station. However, the PRS would determine how the candidates might react to the small living space (only ten by thirteen feet) aboard the shuttle. McAuliffe said this was the most difficult experience of the training. Still, she passed this test, too.

## The Search Ends

The top ten teachers returned to Washington, D.C., in the summer of 1985, for final interviews. Here, the results of their tests and interviews were judged by a panel of seven senior NASA officials. This panel would select a winner and a runner-up for the Teacher in Space program. Both candidates would undergo the training necessary to prepare for the space shuttle mission 51-L, which was scheduled to launch on January 22, 1986.

Finally, all the tests and interviews were over. It was time for the judges to name their final choice. On July 19, 1985, news reporters and photographers gathered at the White House. At the last minute, the ceremony was switched from the Oval Office to the Roosevelt Room to accommodate the large crowd. Reporters from CBS, NBC, and ABC were all there. Cable News Network (CNN) wanted to broadcast the announcement live. Important newspapers such as *The Washington Post* and *The New York Times* wanted the announcement on the front page.

The ten finalists entered the room together. President Reagan was in the hospital being treated for cancer at the time, so Vice President George Bush would announce the winner. He stepped forward to tell everyone how NASA had searched the nation for a teacher with what they called the "right stuff." Now, the name of this person was finally going to be announced.

The finalists already knew who the runner-up and the teacher in space would be. They did not feel it would be fair to put one of them on the spot with such a surprise, so they had insisted on knowing the name of the winning candidate before the announcement was made public.

First, Vice President Bush called the name of the runner-up. It was Barbara Morgan, a second-grade teacher from McCall, Idaho. Morgan would train as the alternate to travel aboard the space shuttle. If, for some reason, the winning candidate could not go, Morgan would take his or her place.

Next, it was time for the announcement everyone was waiting for. The winner was Christa McAuliffe, social studies teacher from Concord, New Hampshire. The vice president smiled and shook hands with McAuliffe as he congratulated her. McAuliffe was given a trophy of a student looking up to a teacher, who was pointing to the stars.

*Christa McAuliffe (left), NASA's teacher in space, posed for this photograph with her alternate, Barbara Morgan. Both women would soon begin a rigorous training schedule to prepare for the* Challenger *flight.*

McAuliffe had to think of something to say. The world was watching her on television and all attention in the room was focused on her. "You would never think that a teacher would be at a loss for words!" she said. "I've made nine wonderful friends over the last two weeks, and when the shuttle goes up, there might be one body but there'll be ten souls that I'm taking with me."[6]

The other nine finalists hugged and congratulated McAuliffe. They had come to know her during the two weeks of competition. They knew she would make an excellent representative of teachers everywhere.

Later that day, a news conference was held on the north lawn of the White House. McAuliffe was asked how it felt to be chosen. "I'm still kind of floating," she said. "I don't know when I'll come down to earth."[7]

Although the finalists for the Teacher in Space program had included both men and women, reporters asked why there had been no African Americans or Hispanics chosen. McAuliffe pointed out that the application process was totally color-blind. There had been no place on the application for mention of race.

Finally, all the interviews were over for the day. McAuliffe called her husband. She could not wait to fly back to New Hampshire to see her family. She left that evening, and although it was rather late when she arrived at the airport, news reporters, family, friends, and a crowd of well-wishers greeted her. The next day, McAuliffe rode in a convertible in a parade down the main street of Concord.

August 6 was named Christa McAuliffe Day in Concord. On that day, McAuliffe received a commendation from the state and city and signed autographs. She even led Nevers' Band—a volunteer orchestra—as it played "Stars and Stripes Forever."

Magazines and newspapers around the world printed articles about McAuliffe. She was invited to appear on numerous television and radio shows. She became very busy with speaking engagements and other presentations. From now on, life would be much different for Christa McAuliffe. She was no longer just a teacher from Concord, New Hampshire. She was now NASA's teacher in space.

# THE CHALLENGER CREW PREPARES

One of the biggest drawbacks of becoming the first teacher in space was the amount of time McAuliffe would be away from her family. She would leave for training in September and come home only for occasional visits until the flight launched in January. After that, she would be busy traveling around the country for several more months, telling the world about her flight aboard the shuttle. Before she left to begin training, McAuliffe tried to get things in order at home.

"I have to take care of the little mundane things because I'll be a much more alert and interested person in Houston if I know everything's all right at home," she said.[1]

She arranged for child care for Scott, who would soon be nine, and six-year-old Caroline. Jane Cogswell, the wife of the school principal, would pick them up after school and watch them until Steve finished work each evening. McAuliffe taught her husband the children's day-to-day routine. She stocked up on groceries, and also made sure that Scott and Caroline had plenty of back-to-school clothes and Steve had plenty of shirts.

She also had to prepare Concord High School for a substitute, since she would be taking leave for the school year. At least she did not have to worry about who that substitute would be. A woman named Eileen O'Hara had already volunteered to take McAuliffe's place in the classroom while she was gone. O'Hara had a similar teaching style. She had also agreed to handle many of McAuliffe's extracurricular activities. McAuliffe helped O'Hara get ready to take over her classroom duties, then she looked for someone to substitute teach her Sunday school class.

At last, McAuliffe had everything ready. Her family would be able to manage for a while without her. Still, it was not easy saying good-bye. Her son, Scott, who would be entering third grade, seemed confused about where his mother was going. Daughter Caroline was not happy at all that McAuliffe would be away again. In addition to all her worries about leaving her family, McAuliffe was nervous about meeting her new crewmates.

## Meeting the Crew

Although the country accepted McAuliffe as the first teacher in space, she worried about how her fellow crew members would accept her. After all, Scobee, Resnik, Smith, McNair, and Onizuka had trained for years to ride the shuttle, and she was only starting her training. She wondered whether they would take her seriously. She knew the other crew members would all work hard to get ready for this mission. She was determined to work just as hard as they did.

McAuliffe met the *Challenger* crew (all but Gregory Jarvis, who had not yet been selected for this particular mission) on September 11, 1985, in Houston. She was ready to begin training. She was feeling a bit anxious, but she knew Francis "Dick" Scobee, the mission commander, accepted her when he said, "No matter what happens, this will always be remembered as the teacher-in-space mission, and you should be proud of that."[2]

## Mission Specialist Judith Resnik

The only other woman aboard mission 51-L would be thirty-six-year-old Judith Resnik. Resnik was a single, dark-haired woman from Akron, Ohio. She was a very private, serious, and hardworking person who did not joke much with others. Growing up, she had been a straight-A student at Firestone High School, and the only girl in the mathematics club. She was also an accomplished pianist, but had decided not to make music her career. "I never play anything softly," she said when questioned about her intensity at the piano.[3]

Instead, she became an electrical engineer, earning a bachelor's degree from Carnegie-Mellon University and a doctorate from the University of Maryland. She was in the first group of women astronauts, selected from more than eight thousand applicants for the space program. She began her training in March 1978.

*Judith Resnik, the other woman aboard the* Challenger, *was one of the first women astronauts.*

Resnik was the second American woman to fly in space. She logged 144 hours and 57 minutes in orbit on mission 41-D, the first flight of the orbiter *Discovery* in 1984. For mission 51-L, Resnik would be one of three mission specialists. She would use the ship's huge robot arm to launch the *Spartan-Halley* satellite that was designed to study Halley's comet.

Resnik realized that a teacher in space could do a lot to interest the American people in the space program once again, but she worried about allowing untrained people into space. Missions were too costly, too technical, and too dangerous to allow civilians aboard for the purpose of publicity. Referring to non-astronauts traveling aboard the shuttle, Resnik had once said to a friend, "What are we going to *do* with these people?"[4] However, she soon recognized that McAuliffe would add more than publicity to the mission. During the months of training, the two women would become friends.

## Commander Dick Scobee

The commander of mission 51-L was Dick Scobee, forty-six, from Cle Elum, Washington. Scobee had graduated from high school in Auburn, Washington, in 1957, then enlisted in the United States Air Force. He trained as a mechanic but really wanted to fly. He took night courses, and in 1965, completed a bachelor of science degree in aerospace engineering from the University of Arizona. This enabled him to receive an

*Dick Scobee, as commander of the* Challenger, *had the authority to stop the flight, but was unaware of the extreme hazards he and his crew would face.*

officer's commission and enter the air force pilot training program.

He received his pilot's wings in 1966 and began a series of flying assignments with the air force, including a combat tour in Vietnam. He had married June Kent of San Antonio, Texas, and they had two children, Kathie and Richard, in the early 1960s. By the time of the *Challenger* mission, Richard and Kathie were in their early twenties. Kathie was married and the mother of a baby. Richard was a senior at the Air Force Academy.

Dick Scobee attended the United States Air Force Aerospace Research Pilot School at Edwards Air Force Base, California, in 1972. After that, he was involved in several test programs. As an air force test pilot, he flew more than forty-five types of aircraft, logging more than sixty-five hundred hours of flight time.

In 1978, Scobee entered NASA's astronaut corps. He was the pilot of STS-41-C, the fifth orbital flight of the *Challenger* spacecraft—launched from Kennedy Space Center, Florida, on April 6, 1984. During this seven-day mission, the crew successfully retrieved and repaired the ailing *Solar Maximum Mission* satellite and returned it to orbit. This was an enormously important mission, because it demonstrated that the space shuttle could repair satellites in orbit. It was something NASA had been eager to prove.

Scobee was looking forward to flight 51-L. "We have a fairly busy timeline and it's nice to have time to go look out the windows," he said. "I guess one of the things that pleasures me most is to have a quiet time where you can go look out the windows, turn out the lights and look at the stars and the earth and the thunderstorms and things like that."[5]

## Pilot Mike Smith

The pilot for mission 51-L was forty-year-old Mike Smith. Raised on a chicken farm in Beaufort, North Carolina, Smith attended the United States Naval Academy in Annapolis, Maryland. He was an experienced pilot, having flown his first solo flight on his sixteenth birthday. Since then, he had flown more than thirty kinds of airplanes and won many medals for his military service in Vietnam. He had also completed navy test pilot school and become a test pilot.

Mike Smith once told a reporter, "Whenever I was conscious of what I wanted to do, I wanted to fly. I can never remember anything else I wanted to do but flying."[6]

Smith was married to Jane Jarell. Together, they had three children: Scott, seventeen; Allison, fourteen; and Erin, eight.

Smith was selected for the space program in 1980. His first space shuttle flight would be 51-L.

## Mission Specialist Ron McNair

Ronald McNair would be the second of three mission specialists aboard the *Challenger*. McNair had become the second African-American astronaut in space as a member of the crew of *Challenger* in 1984. On that

*Astronaut Michael J. Smith was the pilot of the* Challenger.

mission, his duty had been to launch a communications satellite into orbit. The *Challenger*'s 51-L mission would be his second. His job would be to help launch and retrieve *Spartan-Halley*.

McNair had grown up in Lake City, a small South Carolina town where he was valedictorian of his high school class. He earned his undergraduate degree at North Carolina Agricultural and Technical State University at Greensboro. Later, he went on to complete a doctorate in physics from the Massachusetts Institute of Technology. In 1978, he joined the space program.

McNair was also an athlete. He was a leader in track and football in high school. He had a black belt in karate, winning more than thirty trophies in tournaments. He was also a deacon at his Baptist church in Houston, Texas.

McNair was married to a teacher named Cheryl Moore. They had two children—a baby girl named Joy and a three-year-old son, Reggie. McNair loved jazz and played the saxophone. He was a member of an eighteen-piece swing band made up of space center employees, called Max Q. On his previous mission, McNair took his saxophone with him into space and even played a few songs on it while he floated weightlessly through the shuttle. His saxophone, however, would not be aboard on this trip. Other more important equipment came first.

*Ronald McNair was one of the three mission specialists aboard the* Challenger. *He was also the second African American in space.*

## Mission Specialist Ellison Onizuka

Ellison Onizuka, thirty-nine, was from the big island of Hawaii, where he grew up in a small farming town called Keopu. As a child, he enjoyed scouting and rose to the rank of Eagle Scout in only four years.

Onizuka had been the first Japanese American in space. He and his wife, Lorna, had two daughters—Janelle, sixteen, and Darien, ten. Onizuka would be the third mission specialist on the 51-L mission flight. His job would involve photographing Halley's comet.

Onizuka had wanted to become an astronaut since he was sixteen. He had undergraduate and graduate degrees from the University of Colorado. He had been an air force flight engineer and test pilot for eight years before joining the space program in 1978.

Onizuka had flown a secret military mission on the space shuttle in January 1985. His duties on that flight included tracking instruments during launch and reentry, and launching a Department of Defense satellite, using the shuttle's fifty-foot remote arm. He had carried a pair of chopsticks with him on that flight, as a reminder of his Japanese heritage.[7]

Throughout his eight years with NASA, Onizuka made repeated visits to his home community to work with local scouting and 4-H groups. He once told a group of students, "your education and imagination will carry you to places which we won't believe possible. Make your life count—and the world will be a better place because you tried."[8]

*Ellison Onizuka was the first Japanese American in space. He was a mission specialist assigned to photograph Halley's comet during the* Challenger *flight.*

*Gregory Jarvis, the other civilian aboard the* Challenger, *was an engineer for the Hughes Aircraft Company.*

## Payload Specialist Gregory Jarvis

Though McAuliffe was the only schoolteacher among the crew, she was not the only civilian. Gregory Jarvis was a highly trained engineer who worked for the Hughes Aircraft Company. Jarvis, forty-one, was from Detroit, Michigan. He had earned a bachelor's degree in electrical engineering from the State University of New York at Buffalo and a master's degree in engineering from Northeastern University in Boston. Jarvis was married to Marcia G. Jarboe. Both Jarvis and his wife loved the outdoors. They particularly enjoyed bike riding along the coast near their home in Hermosa Beach, California.

Jarvis was in the United States Air Force from 1969 to 1973. He was not an astronaut, however. He was selected by NASA in 1984 to do a series of experiments on the space shuttle. He was supposed to have gone on an earlier flight, the March 1985 51-D *Discovery* mission, but was bumped by Senator Jake Gain, who received the payload specialist assignment Jarvis would have had. Later, Jarvis was bumped again. This time, Congressman Bill Nelson had taken the payload specialist slot for mission 61-C.

Jarvis did not find out until after McAuliffe was selected that he would be part of the 51-L mission. During training, McAuliffe became very close to Jarvis. They were both civilians and had led similar lives, in comparison to the rest of the crew. The two of them played Trivial Pursuit during the slow periods of their training, and they enjoyed talking about their families.

## Barbara Morgan—Alternate Teacher in Space

Barbara Morgan, the alternate teacher in space, trained alongside McAuliffe in Houston. Morgan had earned a bachelor's degree in human biology in 1973 from Stanford University. In 1974, she had earned a teaching certificate from the College of Notre Dame in Belmont, California. Morgan was married to Clayton Michael Morgan, a novelist and United States Forest Service smoke jumper. To join the space program, Morgan took leave from her job as a second-grade teacher at McCall-Donnelly Elementary School in McCall, Idaho.

Though Morgan would not be aboard the flight, she would serve as a television commentator on the ground as McAuliffe taught her lessons from space. Morgan would describe details of the mission and give additional information about McAuliffe's lessons to viewers on a daily one-hour program called "Mission Watch."

Morgan would later join McAuliffe in visiting classrooms all over the United States after the flight was completed. They both wanted to share the knowledge they had gained as participants in NASA's Teacher in Space program. They also wanted to encourage students to study mathematics and science, and prepare them for the future.

*United States Congressman Bill Nelson (left) practiced for his future space flight along with Christa McAuliffe (center) and Barbara Morgan (right).*

## The Training Begins

McAuliffe and Morgan had much to learn. As they began their months of training, they were given stacks of workbooks to read. They would need to learn what the shuttle looked like inside and out. They would have to learn more details about the objectives of mission 51-L. The workbooks instructed them how to read procedures, how to enter and exit the space shuttle, how to operate the equipment in the galley (kitchen area), how to use the cameras that would be on board, and even how to use the bathroom in space.

McAuliffe and Morgan spent hours in a training jet, to get used to the feeling of weightlessness. They

*Christa McAuliffe prepares to try on a space helmet.*

practiced moving around in the crowded cabin of the shuttle orbiter. They took their workbooks home to study every night.

## McAuliffe's Lessons From Space

In addition to learning about the shuttle and space travel in general, Christa McAuliffe had to plan her space lessons. Students all over the country would watch her on closed-circuit television on the sixth day of the flight.

McAuliffe planned two fifteen-minute lessons from space. The first lesson was called "The Ultimate Field

Trip." She would give students a tour of the space shuttle, describing what was done in each area. The lesson would begin on the flight deck. She would introduce Commander Dick Scobee and pilot Mike Smith. Next, she would show viewers *Challenger*'s controls, computers, and cargo bay. After moving to the mid-deck, she would point out the galley, sleeping quarters, and personal hygiene areas.

*Christa McAuliffe undergoes training for her space flight, familiarizing herself with some of the* Challenger*'s equipment.*

The second lesson would be called "Where We've Been, Where We're Going, and Why." At the beginning of this lesson, McAuliffe planned to tell students about the history and future of space flight. She would use models of the Wright brothers' airplane and of the space station NASA planned to build in the coming years, pointing out that only eighty-two years had passed between the first daring flight at Kitty Hawk, North Carolina, and the modern adventures in space of the 1980s. She would also describe the reasons people wanted to live and work in space. She would talk about advantages and disadvantages of processing materials and manufacturing medicines and other items in space. She would give demonstrations to show the effects of near-zero gravity on different objects. She would also talk about important new products and knowledge that have resulted from our exploration of space. She also planned to cover aspects of astronomy, earth observations, the communications satellite launched from *Challenger*, and the *Spartan-Halley* experiment to study Halley's comet.

Three experiments prepared by students who participated in the Shuttle Student Involvement Program (SSIP) would also be on board *Challenger*. The SSIP was designed to help generate interest in the space program by encouraging students to apply to have their science experiments selected for the space shuttle. Three such experiments had been on previous *Challenger* flights. Three more would be on flight 51-L. One of these would observe the development of chicken embryos in space. Another would look at the effects of weightlessness on grain formation and strength in metals. The third student experiment would be about crystal growth.

McAuliffe also planned some demonstrations for schoolchildren who would be watching from their classrooms across the country. For one of the demonstrations, she would use a toy car and some billiard balls as props to explain Isaac Newton's three laws of motion.

McAuliffe would also perform experiments about electromagnetism, showing how magnetic materials are attracted differently in near-zero gravity. She would also demonstrate how simple machines such as the pulley and screw are used in space. She would try to remove a screw from a piece of wood with a screwdriver. Students would see that, without her feet strapped in place, only her body would turn, not the screw.

The most important experiment McAuliffe planned to do in space was to demonstrate a method of plant growth called hydroponics. She would grow bean sprouts without soil, using liquid nutrients. Both the Soviet Union and the United States had grown plants in soil in space by this time. But scientists wondered whether plants would grow as well in space with only liquid nutrients.

Every day during the flight, McAuliffe was to check the growth of six mung bean plants. One of the plants would be sprayed with a mist of nutrients. The other five plants would be growing directly in nutrient solution. At the same time, on Earth, six plants would be grown under identical conditions, except for the effects of gravity. These plants would later be compared to those McAuliffe would bring back from space.

## Americans Get Interested in Space Again

As plans for the Teacher in Space program became more detailed, it was apparent that Americans were getting excited about the space program once again. They were eager for this teacher to make the next shuttle voyage. McAuliffe said, "A lot of people thought it was over when we reached the Moon. They put space on the back burner. But people have a connection with teachers. Now that a teacher has been selected, they are starting to watch the launches again."[9]

Finally, all the training was over. It was time for what McAuliffe and everyone had been waiting for. It was time to launch.

# PREPARING FOR LAUNCH

With fifteen flights scheduled in just over eleven months, 1986 was to be NASA's most ambitious year of shuttle operations to that time. Fourteen of those flights would be from Cape Canaveral. The first mission to launch from the new shuttle port at California's Vandenberg Air Force Base was to take place in 1986, too.

NASA had declared the shuttle "operational" after only four test flights in 1981 and 1982. "Operational" officially meant that the shuttle was ready to begin taking paying customers back and forth from space. For this reason, most members of the public believed the shuttle was now a safe, reliable means of space transport. Many people who were not astronauts wanted to become passengers on such a vehicle. Already, congressmen, a Saudi prince, a Mexican engineer, several aerospace contractor engineers, a French pilot, and even a Canadian Navy officer had flown on the shuttle. Soon the first teacher in space would fly aboard the *Challenger* 51-L mission. With so many non-astronauts flying aboard the shuttle, the public began to believe that space travel really was becoming routine.

## NASA Works Overtime

As the space program entered its busiest year, such an ambitious flight schedule was bound to test NASA's capabilities. Launch crews were working twenty-hour days, seven days a week, with individuals rotating out of the crews for rest. A push was on to keep flights on schedule. With such pressure, workers were bound to make mistakes. But surely NASA officials would never sacrifice safety for political gain. Or would they?

According to a later report on the *Challenger* disaster, "As the flight rate increased, the . . . safety, reliability, and quality assurance work force was decreasing, which adversely affected mission safety."[1]

*Members of the* Challenger *crew receive instructions for their flight.*

However, the public did not know this. Americans thought everything was fine and that shuttle flights were about as safe as regular commercial airliners.

## The Shuttle Program Is Criticized

That same year, academic scientists criticized the space shuttle. They pointed out that, because so much of NASA's budget was now devoted to the shuttle program, seventeen major science projects had been cut or greatly reduced. As a result, the United States had taken an embarrassing third place behind the Soviets and the Europeans when it came to observing Halley's comet.

NASA officials were upset by such criticism. The United States certainly did not want it to appear that the Soviets were ahead of them again. They remembered what an embarrassment *Sputnik* had been. A March 6 mission was planned for the space shuttle *Columbia*. It would allow United States astronauts to observe Halley's comet before the Soviets' *Vega II* spacecraft would encounter the comet on March 9.

However, if 1986 was supposed to be the year of the space shuttle, it was not starting out well at all. *Columbia*, the first orbiter in NASA's shuttle fleet, was due to launch in early January. Problem after problem occurred. Seven times in twenty-five days, *Columbia* was scheduled to enter space. And seven times the launch was canceled.

With only three usable shuttles (the first of the four shuttles, the *Enterprise*, was only used for spare parts) and a long turnaround time between missions, it looked as if NASA's ambitious schedule were already unattainable. But officials ignored the complaints and jabs of newsmen and journalists and kept working to get *Columbia* off the ground. Finally, on January 12, 1986, just two weeks before *Challenger* was scheduled to launch, *Columbia* made it into space. NASA would need *Columbia* to return safely and on time from this mission, and *Challenger* would have to have a trouble-free flight for the next *Columbia* mission, scheduled for March, to launch on time.

## Preparing the Shuttle for Flight

The space shuttle is a complicated space vehicle that has three basic functions. It must launch like a rocket, orbit like a spacecraft, and land like an aircraft. To be able to do all this, the shuttle has three main parts. The part that carries the astronauts and looks like an airplane is called the orbiter. It returns to Earth with the crew and lands like an aircraft.

At liftoff, the orbiter rides piggyback on the huge fuel tank, the second main part of the shuttle. This huge external fuel tank (which is actually made up of two tanks) helps boost the shuttle to an altitude of seventy miles. At that point, the external tank breaks away from the orbiter. The tank is designed to burn up in the atmosphere. Some small fragments fall like meteorites, in remote areas of the Indian Ocean.

Attached to either side of the fuel tank are two solid rocket boosters, which make up the third basic part of the shuttle. These rocket boosters carry millions of tons of fuel. Each one is fifteen stories tall and is made of steel panels that are sealed together by rubber O-rings. As the orbiter reaches a certain altitude during a launch, the rocket boosters are jettisoned from the external fuel tank, using explosive bolts, and are parachuted into the ocean. There, they are picked up by a recovery ship so they can be reused. The boosters recovered from flights prior to *Challenger* mission 51-L showed signs that hot gases had burned partway through the O-rings. If the gases burned completely through the O-rings, it could be disastrous. Flame could escape through the gap and burn part of the shuttle or the huge external tank. If a hole were burned in the external tank, its fuel would leak. The whole shuttle could explode, killing everyone on board.

The solid rocket boosters were made by the Morton Thiokol Company. In July 1985, one of the company's engineers, Roger Boisjoly, sent the managers a memo that warned them about the O-ring problem. "It is my honest and very real fear that if we do not take immediate action to solve the problem . . . then we stand in jeopardy of losing a flight, along with all the launchpad facilities," he wrote. "The result would be a catastrophe of the highest order—loss of human life."[2]

The O-ring damage had been worse when shuttles were launched in colder weather. The coldest launch so far had been at 53°F.

A task force was created at Morton Thiokol in August 1985 to redesign the seals. But the problem was not considered serious enough to ground the shuttle missions. Eventually, managers of Morton Thiokol left out potential O-ring failure from monthly problem reports. The problem was no longer always addressed at flight-readiness meetings. No one considered the O-rings a problem anymore—not the engineering contractors such as Thiokol, not NASA Center's Project Offices, or the National Space Transportation Office & NASA Center Directors, or senior NASA management. The problem had been "closed out," meaning it was considered solved.

On the morning of January 8, 1986, *Challenger* stood on Launch Pad 39B of the Kennedy Space Center. In just over two weeks, the shuttle was scheduled to fly its tenth mission. Technicians in white coveralls worked on several levels of the craft, getting it ready for launch. Checks would be completed to verify that every system was in proper working order.

## Potential Problems

Within the three basic parts of the space shuttle are more than seven hundred separate pieces of flight hardware that are listed as "Criticality 1." This means that the failure of any one would result in the destruction of the shuttle and death of the crew. For this reason, there was a series of four checks and rechecks, called Flight Readiness Reviews (Levels IV, III, II, and I), that was supposed to guarantee that all parts of the shuttle were in proper working order before a launch.

On the afternoon of January 15, senior NASA officials at Cape Canaveral; in Washington, D.C., at the Marshall Space Flight Center; and at the Johnson Space Center in Houston assembled (via conference call) for the Level I Flight Readiness Review. This was the final routine review. All the government officials and aerospace contractors involved with the shuttle's subcomponents were required to present their evidence that the vehicle, its payload (materials and equipment on board), and the ground-support equipment needed to launch and land the shuttle either were or were not ready for a safe flight. *Challenger* passed Flight Readiness Review, Level I—the shuttle was ready for a safe flight. The only concern at the time was that the weather at the scheduled launch time on January 23 could be a potential problem.

Though winter was usually a dry time for Florida, January had been very rainy there that year. If the rain continued, *Columbia*'s return to Kennedy could be delayed and *Challenger*'s launch might have to be rescheduled. The shuttle simply could not fly in rain. At shuttle speeds of over 300 knots (nautical miles per hour), raindrops acted like steel bullets, breaking the delicate tiles that covered the orbiter and protected it from incineration during the blazing heat of reentry.

## Additional Pressure to Launch

There was even more pressure to launch the shuttle *Challenger* on time. President Reagan was scheduled to deliver his State of the Union message on the evening of January 28. The theme of this year's speech was optimism about America's future. NASA wanted the president to include information about upcoming plans for the space program as well as give a detailed description of Christa McAuliffe's *Challenger* flight. NASA suggested that President Reagan

> restate his commitment to the completion of the Space Station by 1994; mention the initiation of the Aerospace Plane Research program; acknowledge the importance of space science; and comment on the flight that was expected to be in orbit at the time he was speaking. . . .[3]

If the *Challenger* were not in flight by the time the president was ready to give his speech, the speech would have to be changed. Neither NASA nor the president wanted that to happen.

## More Problems

Things were not going well. *Columbia* did not return on time. It was three days late, because of weather conditions. This delayed the launch for *Challenger*.

Next, a dust storm in the Sahara Desert further delayed the launch. If an emergency developed several minutes into launch, the *Challenger* crew would have to attempt a landing at a two-mile stretch of concrete in Dakar, Senegal. They would not be able to do this if they could not see the runway through clouds of sand.

The *Challenger* launch was rescheduled for Sunday, January 25. But by Saturday night, January 24, NASA issued a bulletin that warned of an approaching cold

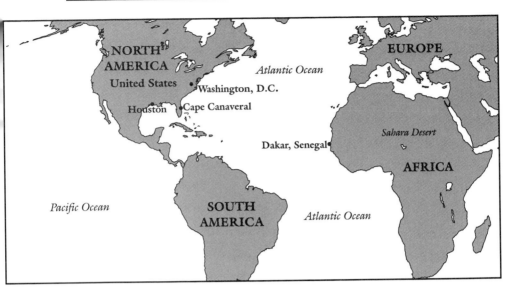

*Some of the shuttle's awesome power can be understood by considering that a flight lifting off from Cape Canaveral, Florida, is expected to make an emergency landing— minutes after launching—in Dakar, Senegal—a flight that would take several hours for an ordinary airplane.*

front that was threatening to deliver rain showers and thunderstorms to the area Sunday morning. The launch was now set for liftoff on Monday morning, January 25, at 9:37.

On Monday, the winds gusted to thirty miles an hour. The shuttle would not be able to attempt an emergency landing at the space center in such high winds, so the flight was postponed another twenty-four hours—just in case.

That evening, the weather reports were not good. A record cold front was due. The next morning's 9:38 launch time was in trouble. A shuttle had never been launched at a temperature below 53° F. Still, the pressure to launch was mounting.

At 8:15 P.M. (Eastern Standard Time) a telephone conference took place between engineers for Morton Thiokol and NASA managers at Kennedy Space Center. The Thiokol engineers unanimously recommended that a launch should not be attempted in temperatures below 53°F. However, because they could not provide positive proof that launching in cold temperatures would jeopardize the safety of the crew, managers at Thiokol overruled this recommendation.

Now NASA could launch. Antifreeze was pumped into fluid lines on the launch tower. The launch remained scheduled for the next morning.

## Countdown to Disaster

By Tuesday morning, January 28, the temperature had dipped to 24°F. This low temperature, combined with the wind (called windchill factor), made it feel as if it were actually 10° below zero. The team at the launch-pad grew more and more concerned about the ice they saw. The ground crew had kept the water running to prevent the pipes that fed the fire extinguishing system from freezing, but a pipe froze anyway.

Unaware of any safety concerns regarding the temperature, the crew members began their day the same way they had the day before, when they thought they were going to launch. They filed to the dining room for breakfast. The table was still decorated from the day before with a centerpiece of red and white roses and American flags. The cook had baked a cake that bore the mission logo and all seven names of the crew members. Launch morning breakfasts are a ritual at NASA. The same menu of steak and eggs is always served. This morning was no different.

After breakfast, at 7:30 A.M., the crew received its final weather briefing. Its members were told about the 25°F temperature, the windchill in the single digits, and the ice at the pad. But the wind had weakened and the sky was clear. The crew was encouraged. They went to their rooms and dressed in their flight overalls and boots. Ellison Onizuka folded up a warm blue flight jacket and had it sent ahead to be waiting for him in the van that would take him to the launchpad.

Everything and everyone who entered the orbiter had to be perfectly clean. The crew had been kept away, or quarantined, from everyone but their closest family members for the past several days, in an effort to prevent anyone from giving them a cold or other disease. Before entering the orbiter now, they went to the "White Room" about ten stories above the launchpad. Here, technicians helped the astronauts put on their helmets. Then they wiped each astronaut's flight boots.

About two hours before the scheduled liftoff, the crew entered the hatch of *Challenger* to take their seats in the orbiter. Technicians helped them buckle in. Scobee and Smith were in the cockpit seats on the flight deck. Behind Scobee sat Resnik. Onizuka was seated behind Smith. McAuliffe and Jarvis were seated side by side, on the middeck below. McNair sat slightly behind McAuliffe, to her left.

The crew members had packed many personal items for their flight. They were each allowed to take up to twenty-four ounces of mementos and other personal belongings. Additionally, they could each have a portable cassette player with earphones, and up to six tapes for entertainment. McAuliffe had packed her husband's class ring from the Virginia Military Institute, her daughter's cross and chain, and her son's favorite possession—a stuffed toy frog he called "Fleegle," though all the frog's stuffing had to be removed in order to keep within the weight limit of personal possessions.

McAuliffe had also packed two T-shirts. One had the New Hampshire state seal on it. The other said, "I touch the future. I teach." A photograph of the student body at Marian High School and a small pennant from Concord High School were also among the items she would take aboard with her, along with an assortment of miniature flags from different schools and states, as well as fifty American flags. She had included a copy of "High Flight"—a favorite poem of hers, written by a Canadian combat pilot who had died over Great Britain in 1941.

Judith Resnik had packed personal items, too—a ring for her nephew and a heart-shaped locket for her niece. Greg Jarvis planned to carry banners from his alma maters—Northeastern University and the State University of New York at Buffalo.

Christa McAuliffe was dedicated to teaching and believed that her space mission would help encourage her students to learn more about science.

## SOURCE DOCUMENT

*OH, I HAVE SLIPPED THE SURLY BONDS OF EARTH,*
*AND DANCED THE SKIES ON LAUGHTER-SILVERED WINGS;*
*SUNWARD I'VE CLIMBED AND JOINED THE TUMBLING MIRTH*
*OF SUN-SPLIT CLOUDS—AND DONE A HUNDRED THINGS*
*YOU HAVE NOT DREAMED OF—WHEELED AND SOARED AND SWUNG*
*HIGH IN THE SUNLIT SILENCE. HOVERING THERE*
*I'VE CHASED THE SHOUTING WIND ALONG AND FLUNG*
*MY EAGER CRAFT THROUGH FOOTLESS HALLS OF AIR.*
*UP, UP THE LONG DELIRIOUS BURNING BLUE*
*I'VE TOPPED THE WIND-SWEPT HEIGHTS WITH EASY GRACE,*
*WHERE NEVER LARK, OR EVEN EAGLE, FLEW;*
*AND WHILE WITH SILENT LIFTING MIND I'VE TROD*
*THE HIGH UNTRESPASSED SANCTITY OF SPACE,*
*PUT OUT MY HAND, AND TOUCHED THE FACE OF GOD.*[4]

*Christa McAuliffe loved the poem "High Flight" by John Gillespie Magee, Jr. She brought a copy of it with her aboard the* Challenger.

Everything seemed to be ready for the *Challenger*'s flight. The crew members' personal belongings had been packed securely aboard the shuttle, along with all the other equipment they would need to carry out their mission. The *Challenger* crew was strapped in. Soon it would be time to launch.

The parents of Christa McAuliffe, Grace and Ed Corrigan, were so nervous and excited that they were already crying when the *Challenger* lifted off the launchpad that cold morning of January 28. A few minutes later, the Corrigans' NASA escorts had to hold them up as they heard the voice on the loudspeaker solemnly announce, "Flight controllers here [are] looking very carefully at the situation. Obviously a major malfunction. We have no downlink. We have a report from the Flight Dynamics Officer that the vehicle has exploded."[1]

# 6

# AFTER THE TRAGEDY

Soon the escorts led the Corrigans and other families away. In the VIP grandstands, cries turned to wails. The families of the crew were taken to the crew's quarters where they waited.

McAuliffe's husband, Steve, their son, Scott, and daughter, Caroline, sat in McAuliffe's dormitory room, waiting for news. There was nothing else they could do. Barbara Morgan, the alternate teacher in space, obviously shaken, sat in the large living area of the dorm, waiting to help the families of the crew with arrangements and make necessary phone calls to other family members.

*Eager family and friends watched the* Challenger *launch.*

## The World Waits for News

People across the country were in a state of shock. No one could really believe what had just happened. Television networks interrupted regular programs to announce the tragedy and followed the story with live coverage the rest of the day. Videotape of the explosion was played over and over while newsrooms and reporters waited for the latest information from NASA. Finally, at 4:30 P.M., an announcement was made. Associate Administrator for Space Flight at the Kennedy Space Center Jesse Moore said:

*The space shuttle* Challenger *exploded seventy-three seconds after it lifted off.*

> It is with deep, heartfelt sorrow that I address you here this afternoon. At 11:30 A.M. this morning, the space program experienced a national tragedy with the explosion of the space shuttle Challenger approximately a minute and a half after launch from here at the Kennedy Space Center. I regret that I have to report that based on very preliminary search of the ocean where Challenger impacted this morning— these searches have not revealed any evidence that the crew of Challenger survived.[2]

Moore went on to explain what he could about the accident. However, at the time, neither he nor anyone else knew the cause of the fireball and the explosion.

President Reagan immediately sent Vice President George Bush to the Kennedy Space Center. He offered condolences to the families of the astronauts. Senator and former astronaut John Glenn was there, too. He told the families that he had felt a sense of loss, similar to theirs, when the three astronauts (Virgil I. Grissom, Edward H. White II, and Robert B. Chaffee) had died in the *Apollo 1* fire nineteen years before. They had been close friends of his.

President Reagan was to deliver his State of the Union address that evening. Instead, he postponed it for one week and gave a speech that afternoon from the Oval Office in tribute to the *Challenger* astronauts. He told the families of the crew, "Your loved ones were daring and brave, and they had that special grace, that special spirit that says, 'Give me a challenge and I'll meet it with joy.' They had hunger to explore the universe and discover its truths. They wished to serve and

LADIES AND GENTLEMEN, I'D PLANNED TO SPEAK TO YOU TONIGHT TO REPORT ON THE STATE OF THE UNION, BUT THE EVENTS OF EARLIER TODAY HAVE LED ME TO CHANGE THOSE PLANS. TODAY IS A DAY FOR MOURNING AND REMEMBERING. NANCY AND I ARE PAINED TO THE CORE BY THE TRAGEDY OF THE SHUTTLE CHALLENGER. WE KNOW WE SHARE THIS PAIN WITH ALL OF THE PEOPLE OF OUR COUNTRY. THIS IS TRULY A NATIONAL LOSS.

NINETEEN YEARS AGO, ALMOST TO THE DAY, WE LOST THREE ASTRONAUTS IN A TERRIBLE ACCIDENT ON THE GROUND. BUT, WE'VE NEVER LOST AN ASTRONAUT IN FLIGHT; WE'VE NEVER HAD A TRAGEDY LIKE THIS. AND PERHAPS WE'VE FORGOTTEN THE COURAGE IT TOOK FOR THE CREW OF THE SHUTTLE; BUT THEY, THE CHALLENGER SEVEN, WERE AWARE OF THE DANGERS, BUT OVERCAME THEM AND DID THEIR JOBS BRILLIANTLY. WE MOURN SEVEN HEROES: MICHAEL SMITH, DICK SCOBEE, JUDITH RESNIK, RONALD MCNAIR, ELLISON ONIZUKA, GREGORY JARVIS, AND CHRISTA MCAULIFFE. WE MOURN THEIR LOSS AS A NATION TOGETHER. . . .

WE'VE GROWN USED TO WONDERS IN THIS CENTURY. IT'S HARD TO DAZZLE US. BUT FOR TWENTY-FIVE YEARS THE UNITED STATES SPACE PROGRAM HAS BEEN DOING JUST THAT. WE'VE GROWN USED TO THE IDEA OF SPACE, AND PERHAPS WE FORGET THAT WE'VE ONLY JUST BEGUN. WE'RE STILL PIONEERS. THEY, THE MEMBERS OF THE CHALLENGER CREW, WERE PIONEERS. . . .

THERE'S A COINCIDENCE TODAY. ON THIS DAY 390 YEARS AGO, THE GREAT EXPLORER SIR FRANCIS DRAKE DIED ABOARD SHIP OFF THE COAST OF PANAMA. IN HIS LIFETIME THE GREAT FRONTIERS WERE THE OCEANS, AND A HISTORIAN LATER SAID, "HE LIVED BY THE SEA, DIED ON IT, AND WAS BURIED IN IT." WELL, TODAY WE CAN SAY OF THE CHALLENGER CREW: THEIR DEDICATION WAS, LIKE DRAKE'S, COMPLETE. . . .[3]

*Instead of giving his State of the Union message, President Reagan spoke about the terrible tragedy that had occurred.*

they did. They served all of us." President Reagan knew that schoolchildren all across the country had witnessed the tragedy. To them he said,

> I know it is hard to understand, but sometimes painful things like this happen. It's all part of the process of exploration and discovery. It's all part of taking a chance and expanding man's horizons. The future doesn't belong to the fainthearted; it belongs to the brave. The Challenger crew was pulling us into the future, and we'll continue to follow them.

The president ended his speech by saying, "We will never forget them, nor the last time we saw them, this morning, as they prepared for the journey and waved goodbye and 'slipped the surly bonds of earth' to 'touch the face of God.'"[4] Reagan was quoting the poem "High Flight" that McAuliffe had liked so much.

## The World Mourns

Americans everywhere mourned the death of the *Challenger* crew. Flags flew at half-staff. Tributes were planned all over the country to honor the seven space heroes.

On January 30, Christa McAuliffe's alma mater, Framingham State College, held a memorial service. About a thousand people attended. Included were McAuliffe's parents and other family members. Governor Michael Dukakis of Massachusetts and others paid tribute to McAuliffe and the other members of the *Challenger* crew. Following the service, hundreds of students met outside the auditorium. They sang

"America" and released a bouquet of seven black balloons in honor of the *Challenger* astronauts.

The next day, January 31, a memorial service was held at the Johnson Space Center in Houston. Relatives of the astronauts and thousands of NASA employees attended. President and Mrs. Reagan were there, seated between Jane Smith (widow of the *Challenger* pilot) and June Scobee (widow of the commander).

In his eulogy for the seven astronauts, President Reagan named each of them and said, "We will always remember them, these skilled professionals . . . and we will cherish each of their stories—stories of triumph and bravery, stories of true American heroes." The president continued:

> The sacrifice of your loved ones has stirred the soul of our nation and, through the pain, our hearts have been opened to a profound truth—the future is not free, the story of all human progress is one of a struggle against all odds. We learned again that this America . . . was built by men and women like our seven star voyagers, who answered a call beyond duty, who gave more than was expected or required, and who gave it with little thought to worldly reward.
>
> Sometimes, when we reach for the stars, we fall short. But we must pick ourselves up again and press on. . . . Today, we promise Dick Scobee and his crew that their dream lives on. . . . Man will continue his conquest of space. To reach out for new goals and ever greater achievements—that is the way we shall commemorate our seven Challenger heroes.[5]

The band played "God Bless America." Four NASA T-38 jets thundered one thousand feet overhead in the Missing Man formation that symbolizes the loss of a pilot. Just before they flew above the crowd, one plane left the other three, zooming ahead, faster and higher.

President Reagan shook hands and offered condolences to McAuliffe's husband and parents and the other relatives of the *Challenger* crew. Both he and his wife, Nancy, offered words of comfort to the astronauts' children. The families of the crew moved to another building, where they got the chance to speak to each other.

Senator Edward Kennedy attended the service. Shortly after it was over, he sent a message to McAuliffe's family, saying that he, Caroline, and John (his niece and nephew—children of the late President John F. Kennedy) would like to pay their respects, if the family would not mind meeting them in another room.

When the Kennedys and McAuliffe's parents met, Caroline said, "Your daughter was an inspiration to me." McAuliffe's father, Ed, replied, "And your father inspired Christa."[6]

There were many other tributes to McAuliffe and the rest of the *Challenger* crew. Students at Concord High School, where McAuliffe had taught, held a memorial assembly the same day as the ceremonies in Houston. The president of the student council read a two-page letter from President Reagan.

In McAuliffe's hometown of Concord, New Hampshire, people gathered at the State House plaza on the night of January 31 to pay tribute to McAuliffe. Only one month before, many of these same people had come here to celebrate New Year's Eve and to watch McAuliffe judge a snow sculpture contest with the theme "Reach for the Stars." The mood was very different on this cold night. Seven bells tolled from the tower of St. Paul's Church in memory of the seven astronauts.

A service was held at the Kennedy Space Center in Florida on February 1. NASA employees there wanted to pay their respects to the *Challenger* astronauts. A large wreath of white carnations was dropped from a helicopter into the Atlantic Ocean where the debris from the *Challenger* had rained down from the sky that terrible day.

Two days later, a private funeral mass was attended by Christa McAuliffe's family at St. Peter's Church in Concord, New Hampshire. Family and friends, including Barbara Morgan, the alternate for the Teacher in Space program, came to pay tribute to McAuliffe.

A nationwide flag-raising ceremony was coordinated by the Kentucky Department of Education. On February 4, at 11:39 A.M., exactly one week after the *Challenger* exploded, education officials at sites in more than thirty states raised "the flag of learning and liberty"—the first flag to symbolize the link between education and a strong free nation—to commemorate the importance of public education. Christa McAuliffe had carried small versions of this flag with her on the shuttle. She had planned to distribute them after the flight.

Many states started scholarship funds in McAuliffe's memory to help students who wanted to become teachers. In New Hampshire, at a ceremony on February 7, Governor John Sununu announced the formation of a "living memorial" trust fund. Every year, it would allow one New Hampshire teacher a year-long leave from the classroom to explore studies outside his or her field. The program would keep alive the meaning of McAuliffe's mission by promoting the love of knowledge and spirit of discovery in dedicated teachers. The fund was approved by members of McAuliffe's family, who attended the announcement

*The remains of the* Challenger *crew were taken from Kennedy Space Center to the Dover Air Force Base in Delaware, before the individual crew members were laid to rest in private ceremonies.*

ceremony. A family member would help direct the fund. The first representative to do so would be McAuliffe's mother, Grace Corrigan.

At the first full session of the House of Representatives in New Hampshire, the members stood silently in honor of Christa McAuliffe and her lost crewmates. Representative Gary Ackerman of New York introduced legislation in the United States House of Representatives in Washington, D.C., to designate January 28, the day of the tragedy, National Teachers' Recognition Day.

After the many tributes and memorials to the *Challenger* astronauts were conducted, it was time to find the cause of the accident and decide what to do about continuing and improving the shuttle program. In February, President Reagan named a presidential commission whose mission would be to do just that— investigate the cause of the *Challenger* tragedy so that NASA could correct the problem and the space shuttle could fly once again.

# 7

# THE INVESTIGATION

The commission to investigate the cause of the *Challenger* disaster quickly got under way. Former Secretary of State William P. Rogers headed the commission, and soon it was referred to as the Rogers Commission. Other members included Neil Armstrong (the first man to walk on the moon) and Sally Ride (the first American woman in space), as well as many other prominent space experts and engineers.

## The Commission's Purpose

The president directed the commission to review the circumstances surrounding the accident. Its members were to establish the probable cause or causes of the accident, and to develop recommendations for corrective or other action.[1]

The commission was to submit its final report to the president and the administrator of NASA within 120 days of the order. The investigation was an awesome task. At that point, all the commission had were a few pieces of debris and flight data. Finding the cause of the accident would take the time, energy, and hard work of many people.

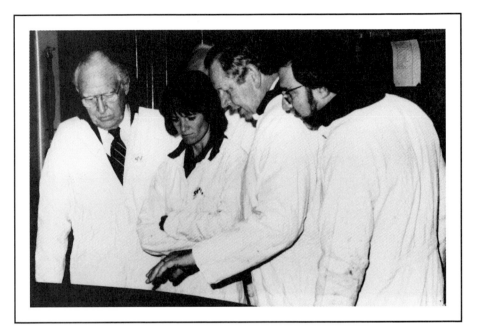

*President Reagan called for a commission to investigate the* Challenger *explosion. The commission included astronaut Sally Ride (second from left).*

Members of the commission divided into four investigative panels: a Development and Production Panel responsible for investigating the way materials for the shuttle were purchased, tested, and evaluated; a Pre-Launch Activities Panel to assess the shuttle system processing, launch readiness process, and pre-launch security; a Mission Planning and Operations Panel to investigate crew safety areas; and an Accident Analysis Panel to analyze the data recovered from the accident.

In addition to the work of the commission, NASA conducted its own investigation of the accident. The military and the National Transportation Safety Board

### WILLIAM P. ROGERS, CHAIRMAN

FORMER SECRETARY OF STATE UNDER PRESIDENT NIXON (1969–1973), AND ATTORNEY GENERAL UNDER PRESIDENT EISENHOWER (1957–1961), CURRENTLY A PRACTICING ATTORNEY AND SENIOR PARTNER IN THE LAW FIRM OF ROGERS & WELLS. . . .

### NEIL A. ARMSTRONG, VICE CHAIRMAN

. . . MR. ARMSTRONG WAS SPACECRAFT COMMANDER FOR APOLLO 11, JULY 16–24, 1969, THE FIRST MANNED LUNAR LANDING MISSION. . . .

### DAVID C. ACHESON

FORMER SENIOR VICE PRESIDENT AND GENERAL COUNSEL, COMMUNICATIONS SATELLITE CORPORATION (1967–1974), CURRENTLY A PARTNER IN THE LAW FIRM OF DRINKER BIDDLE & REATH. . . .

### DR. EUGENE E. COVERT

. . . MEMBER OF THE NATIONAL ACADEMY OF ENGINEERING, HE WAS A RECIPIENT OF THE EXCEPTIONAL CIVILIAN SERVICE AWARD, USAF, IN 1973 AND THE NASA PUBLIC SERVICE AWARD IN 1980. HE HOLDS A DOCTORATE IN SCIENCE FROM MASSACHUSETTS INSTITUTE OF TECHNOLOGY.

### DR. RICHARD P. FEYNMAN

. . . NOBEL PRIZE WINNER IN PHYSICS, 1965, HE ALSO RECEIVED THE EINSTEIN AWARD IN 1954, THE OERSTED MEDAL IN 1972 AND THE NIELS BOHR INTERNATIONAL GOLD MEDAL IN 1973. HE HOLDS A DOCTORATE IN PHYSICS FROM PRINCETON (1942).

### ROBERT B. HOTZ

. . . HE WAS THE EDITOR-IN-CHIEF OF AVIATION WEEK & SPACE TECHNOLOGY MAGAZINE (1953–1980). HE SERVED IN THE AIR FORCE IN WORLD WAR II AND WAS AWARDED THE AIR MEDAL WITH OAK LEAF CLUSTER. SINCE 1982, HE HAS BEEN A MEMBER OF THE GENERAL ADVISORY COMMITTEE TO THE ARMS CONTROL AND DISARMAMENT AGENCY.

*The Rogers Commission was made up of many prominent and knowledgeable Americans.*

### MAJOR GENERAL DONALD J. KUTYNA, USAF

. . . A COMMAND PILOT WITH OVER 4,000 FLIGHT HOURS, HE IS A RECIPIENT OF THE DISTINGUISHED SERVICE MEDAL, DISTINGUISHED FLYING CROSS, LEGION OF MERIT AND NINE AIR MEDALS.

### DR. SALLY K. RIDE

. . . BORN IN LOS ANGELES, CALIFORNIA, SHE WAS A MISSION SPECIALIST ON STS-7, LAUNCHED ON JUNE 18, 1983, BECOMING THE FIRST AMERICAN WOMAN IN SPACE. SHE ALSO FLEW ON MISSION 41-G LAUNCHED OCTOBER 5, 1984. SHE HOLDS A DOCTORATE IN PHYSICS FROM STANFORD UNIVERSITY (1978) AND IS STILL AN ACTIVE ASTRONAUT.

### ROBERT W. RUMMEL

. . . HE IS A MEMBER OF THE NATIONAL ACADEMY OF ENGINEERING AND IS HOLDER OF THE NASA DISTINGUISHED PUBLIC SERVICE MEDAL.

### JOSEPH F. SUTTER

[H]E HAS BEEN WITH BOEING SINCE 1945 AND WAS A PRINCIPAL FIGURE IN THE DEVELOPMENT OF THREE GENERATIONS OF JET AIRCRAFT. IN 1984, HE WAS ELECTED TO THE NATIONAL ACADEMY OF ENGINEERING. . . .

### DR. ARTHUR B. C. WALKER, JR.

. . . [A] MEMBER OF THE AMERICAN PHYSICAL SOCIETY, AMERICAN GEOPHYSICAL UNION, AND THE AMERICAN ASTRONOMY SOCIETY. HE HOLDS A DOCTORATE IN PHYSICS FROM THE UNIVERSITY OF ILLINOIS (1962).

### DR. ALBERT D. WHEELON

. . . HE WAS THE FIRST PERSON TO PENETRATE THE SOUND BARRIER AND THE FIRST TO FLY AT A SPEED OF MORE THAN 1,600 MILES AN HOUR.

### DR. ALTON G. KEEL, JR., EXECUTIVE DIRECTOR

. . . BORN IN NEWPORT NEWS, VIRGINIA, HE HOLDS A DOCTORATE IN ENGINEERING PHYSICS FROM THE UNIVERSITY OF VIRGINIA (1970).[2]

were also involved. These organizations conducted the salvage and analysis of the shuttle wreckage.

## The Commission's Findings

The commission soon identified the technical cause of the accident. The explosion of the $1.2 billion space-craft was due to a faulty O-ring seal on the solid rocket fuel booster—a $900 synthetic rubber band that engineers had warned was vulnerable at low temperatures. The Rogers Commission found both the company that made the O-rings—Morton Thiokol—and NASA itself guilty of allowing an avoidable accident to occur.

Photographs and videotape of the launch were studied closely. They showed a fire plume escaping from the right solid rocket booster. The flame burned through the bottom connecting strut that held the booster to the external tank. The top of the booster swung into this tank and punctured it. Super-cooled liquid oxygen and liquid hydrogen gushed out of the punctured tank. When the two flammable liquids were exposed to flame, an explosion occurred, ripping both the tank and the shuttle to pieces.

The commission and the public were greatly disturbed by other information discovered about the O-rings. The commission stated that "neither Thiokol nor NASA responded adequately to internal warnings about faulty seal design," though they had been warned nearly three years before.[3]

Naturally, the families of the crew were angry. "It shouldn't have happened," said McAuliffe's mother.

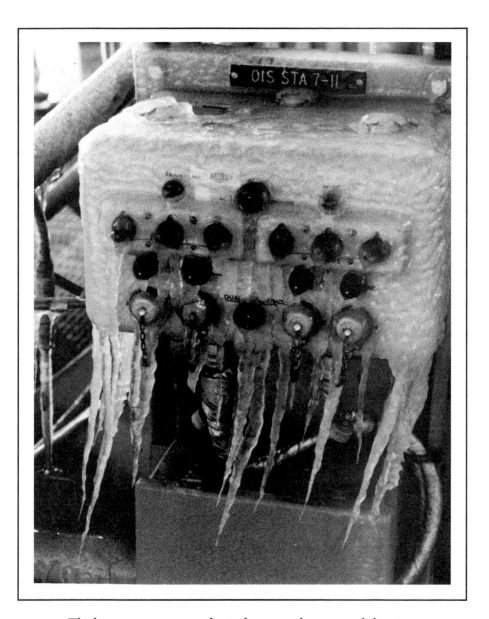

*The low temperature and windy atmosphere caused the pipes that fed the fire extinguishing system of* Challenger *to freeze.*

"They were told not to launch, and they decided, 'Twenty-four other shuttle flights went off O.K.' They were complacent."[4]

Sally Ride, the only active shuttle astronaut on the Rogers Commission, was particularly disturbed. "I am not ready to fly again now," she told an interviewer. "I think there are very few astronauts who are ready to fly again now." She said that NASA needed to understand its own problems and fix them. Ride also questioned whether private citizens were really ready to go into space: "I think we may have been misleading people into thinking that this is a routine operation, that it is just like getting on an airliner and going across the country, and that it's that safe. It's not."[5]

## The Fate of the Crew

The investigation also included determining how the crew members died. At first, everyone assumed that the crew had been killed instantly in the explosion. But a study of photographs showed that the crew compartment had come out of the blast in nearly one piece. On March 8, divers located the crew compartment in about one hundred feet of water, eighteen miles east of the *Challenger*'s launchpad.

In early April, reporters were allowed inside a hangar at the Kennedy Space Center. Here, shuttle debris had been collected and laid out on a huge grid in the shape of the *Challenger*. The crew compartment was being examined in another hangar that reporters were never allowed to visit. However, the reporters learned that physical evidence showed that, at the time the crew compartment hit the water, all crew members had probably still been strapped in their seats.

By April 18, identifiable remains from all seven crew members had been found. Doctors worked for weeks, trying to learn the cause of death, to determine how long the crew had survived after the orbiter broke up. The findings were inconclusive. However, several things were learned from the wreckage.

It is certain that the forces of the breakup were not violent enough to cause death or even unconsciousness, so it is unlikely that the astronauts died from the explosion. The crew compartment was outfitted with seven emergency air packs. Each member of the crew had an air pack to use if the crew compartment lost breathable air for some reason or other, such as fire or depressurization. These air packs had to be turned on by hand. Four of the seven emergency air packs were recovered. Three of them had been used. The fourth air pack was not turned on and was identified as belonging to Commander Dick Scobee. More than half the oxygen in the three activated packs had been used up. It took the compartment two and a half minutes to fall to the water. This means that, during the fall, at least three of the astronauts were breathing.

One of the packs was Mike Smith's. His pack had been mounted behind his cockpit seat. This means that it was turned on by one of the other astronauts, probably Ellison Onizuka, who was seated behind Smith.

*The Rogers Commission analyzed the wreckage from the* Challenger *explosion that had been retrieved from the Atlantic Ocean.*

Although at least three members of the crew were breathing, it does not mean they were conscious. If any part of the crew compartment were damaged or punctured by the explosion, the cabin would have quickly depressurized. If the cabin lost air pressure at that altitude (47,000 feet), the crew, with or without air packs, would have lost consciousness moments later.

The crew compartment probably hit the water about two minutes and forty-five seconds after the breakup, at about two hundred miles an hour. If any of the crew members were still alive during the fall, he or she would not have survived the impact. On July 28, 1986, Joseph P. Kerwin, a biomedical specialist from the Johnson Space Center in Houston, Texas, sent a letter to Admiral Richard H. Truly, the associate administrator for space flight. The letter stated:

> the cause of death of Challenger astronauts cannot be positively determined; the forces to which the crew were exposed during orbiter breakup were probably not sufficient to cause death or serious injury; and the crew possibly, but not certainly, lost consciousness in the seconds following orbiter breakup due to in-flight loss of crew module pressure.

The letter concluded, "Finally, the skilled and dedicated efforts of the team from the Armed Forces Institute of Pathology, and their expert consultants, could not determine whether in-flight lack of oxygen occurred, nor could they determine the cause of death."[6]

If some or all crew members survived the explosion, then the probable cause of death was the crash into the ocean. In that case, a crew module equipped with escape and parachute systems might have saved them—but only if the orbiter were not tumbling as it dropped from the sky. An escape system of this kind was considered by NASA, but installing such an escape module would require redesign of the orbiter. This would seriously affect the shuttle program's costs and schedules. And, because it was not known for sure whether an escape system would have saved the *Challenger* crew (or future shuttle crews), plans for such a system were ruled out.

## The Commission's Recommendations

The commission issued its report in June 1986. It gave a series of nine recommendations as to what should be done to help make the shuttle safe for future flights.

The most important recommendation was the redesign of the faulty solid rocket motor joints. The rocket motors were designed in sections that had to be assembled at the launch site. The connections between the sections are called joints. These joints contain the O-rings that failed to keep the explosive gasses from leaking on the *Challenger*. The commission called for either a new design that would not need the joints or a redesign of the current joints and seals. The new design would also have to include realistic tests that simulate as closely as possible launch conditions and all operating conditions during shuttle flight.

Recommendation two called for a new system of management of the shuttle program. All funding and program work would be placed under the authority of the national program manager. Before this recommendation, funding and program work was managed at different shuttle centers across the country.

Recommendation three called for a review of all items that needed improvement before the space shuttle would be able to safely fly again.

DEAR MR. PRESIDENT:

ON BEHALF OF THE COMMISSION, IT IS MY PRIVILEGE TO PRESENT THE REPORT OF THE PRESIDENTIAL COMMISSION ON THE SPACE SHUTTLE CHALLENGER ACCIDENT.

SINCE BEING SWORN IN ON FEBRUARY 6, 1986, THE COMMISSION HAS BEEN ABLE TO CONDUCT A COMPREHENSIVE INVESTIGATION OF THE CHALLENGER ACCIDENT. THIS REPORT DOCUMENTS OUR FINDINGS AND MAKES RECOMMENDATIONS FOR YOUR CONSIDERATION.

OUR OBJECTIVE HAS BEEN NOT ONLY TO PREVENT ANY RECURRENCE OF THE FAILURE RELATED TO THIS ACCIDENT, BUT TO THE EXTENT POSSIBLE TO REDUCE OTHER RISKS IN FUTURE FLIGHTS. HOWEVER, THE COMMISSION DID NOT CONSTRUE ITS MANDATE TO REQUIRE A DETAILED EVALUATION OF THE ENTIRE SHUTTLE SYSTEM. IT FULLY RECOGNIZES THAT THE RISK ASSOCIATED WITH SPACE FLIGHT CANNOT BE TOTALLY ELIMINATED.

EACH MEMBER OF THE COMMISSION SHARED THE PAIN AND ANGUISH THE NATION FELT AT THE LOSS OF SEVEN BRAVE AMERICANS IN THE CHALLENGER ACCIDENT ON JANUARY 28, 1986.

THE NATION'S TASK NOW IS TO MOVE AHEAD TO RETURN TO SAFE SPACE FLIGHT AND TO ITS RECOGNIZED POSITION OF LEADERSHIP IN SPACE. THERE COULD BE NO MORE FITTING TRIBUTE TO THE CHALLENGER CREW THAN TO DO SO.

SINCERELY,
WILLIAM P. ROGERS
CHAIRMAN[7]

*This is the letter that the presidential commission enclosed with its report to Ronald Reagan on the* Challenger *disaster.*

*The battered part of* Challenger's *right wing bears witness to the fatal explosion.*

Recommendation four called for the establishment of an office of safety, reliability, and quality assurance. This would ensure that all materials and procedures for the shuttle were safe and reliable.

Recommendation five demanded an end to what the commission called "management isolation." This meant that key information (such as the concern about the O-rings) would be made known before a scheduled flight to everyone involved in the shuttle's safety.

Recommendation six urged NASA to improve landing safety. Regarding tire, brake, and nosewheel steering systems, the commission said, "These systems

THE CONSENSUS OF THE COMMISSION AND PARTICIPATING INVESTIGATIVE AGENCIES IS THAT THE LOSS OF THE SPACE SHUTTLE CHALLENGER WAS CAUSED BY A FAILURE IN THE JOINT BETWEEN THE TWO LOWER SEGMENTS OF THE RIGHT SOLID ROCKET MOTOR. THE SPECIFIC FAILURE WAS THE DESTRUCTION OF THE SEALS THAT ARE INTENDED TO PREVENT HOT GASES FROM LEAKING THROUGH THE JOINT DURING THE PROPELLANT BURN OF THE ROCKET MOTOR. THE EVIDENCE ASSEMBLED BY THE COMMISSION INDICATES THAT NO OTHER ELEMENT OF THE SPACE SHUTTLE SYSTEM CONTRIBUTED TO THIS FAILURE.

IN ARRIVING AT THIS CONCLUSION, THE COMMISSION REVIEWED IN DETAIL ALL AVAILABLE DATA, REPORTS AND RECORDS; DIRECTED AND SUPERVISED NUMEROUS TESTS, ANALYSES, AND EXPERIMENTS BY NASA, CIVILIAN CONTRACTORS AND VARIOUS GOVERNMENT AGENCIES; AND THEN DEVELOPED SPECIFIC FAILURE SCENARIOS AND THE RANGE OF MOST PROBABLE CAUSATIVE FACTORS.

### FINDINGS

1. A COMBUSTION GAS LEAK THROUGH THE RIGHT SOLID ROCKET MOTOR AFT FIELD JOINT INITIATED AT OR SHORTLY AFTER IGNITION EVENTUALLY WEAKENED AND/OR PENETRATED THE EXTERNAL TANK INITIATING VEHICLE STRUCTURAL BREAKUP AND LOSS OF THE SPACE SHUTTLE CHALLENGER DURING STS MISSION 51-L.[8]

*The presidential commission summarized what it believed was the cause of the accident in its report to President Reagan.*

do not have sufficient safety margin, particularly at abort landing sites."[9]

Recommendation seven called upon NASA to "make all efforts to provide a crew escape system for use during controlled gliding flight (landing)."[10]

Recommendation eight stated that NASA must establish a flight rate consistent with its resources. NASA would not be pressured to launch more shuttles than it could safely handle.

Recommendation nine involved Criticality 1 items—those items that absolutely must function properly to avoid disaster. The recommendation called for the establishment of a system of analyzing and reporting the performance of these items.

President Reagan approved the recommendations and directed NASA to carry them out. The priority task of redesigning the solid rocket motor joints and seals was placed under the management of John W. Thomas, the spacelab program office manager at Marshall Space Flight Center in Huntsville, Alabama.

Since the main recommendation of the commission was the redesign of the joints and the O-ring seals connecting the rocket boosters, it was first necessary to test the old design under the same conditions as the day of the actual explosion. In October 1986, those conditions were reproduced in a test situation. The same results occurred—the boosters leaked because the joints did not stay sealed. This meant the true cause of the accident was indeed failure of the joints to stay sealed with the O-rings. Engineers then went to work on the redesign of the joints and the O-ring seals.

The redesign of the joint seal added a third O-ring. Before the redesign there were only two; one acted as a seal, the other was a backup seal. It also eliminated the putty that had served as a partial seal on the original design. Insulation replaced the putty. A capture device was added to prevent or reduce the opening of the joint as the booster inflated under motor gas pressure during ignition. The third O-ring would be added to seal the joint at the capture device. The former O-rings would be replaced by rings of the same size, but made of a better material called fluorosilicone, or nitrile rubber. Heating strips were added around the joints to make sure the O-rings did not experience temperatures lower than 75°F regardless of the surrounding temperature. The gap openings that the O-rings were designed to seal were reduced to six thousandths of an inch from the former gap of thirty thousandths of an inch. John Thomas stated, "We were charged in the redesign effort with two objectives. The primary objective was to design a safe joint and the secondary objective was to utilize existing hardware if we could design a safe joint in that pursuit. I believe we have done that."[11]

## Memorials and Money

About a month after the commission filed its report, another memorial was created in honor of the *Challenger* astronauts. In July 1986, the Astronauts

Memorial Foundation and NASA agreed to establish the astronaut memorial on the grounds of the Kennedy Space Center at Cape Canaveral, Florida. Though the idea for the memorial was conceived after the *Challenger* explosion, the program would honor all those people who have died in the pursuit of space exploration—pilots who had lost their lives in training accidents; astronauts Grissom, White, and Chaffee, who had died so tragically in the *Apollo 1* fire; and the seven people lost when the *Challenger* exploded. The memorial stands by a lagoon at the Visitors Center Complex. Made of polished black granite (forty feet high and fifty feet wide), the astronauts' names have been carved on the granite surface.

The families of Christa McAuliffe, Ellison Onizuka, Gregory Jarvis, and Dick Scobee sued the United States government and Morton Thiokol. They accepted $7.7 million to help compensate for their losses. The sums designated for each family were never revealed, but they were based on the age and number of dependents of the deceased. The families of Ronald McNair and Judith Resnik also sued Morton Thiokol. They settled independently, reportedly for multiple millions. The last suit to be resolved was that of Jane Smith, who filed a $1.5 billion suit against Morton Thiokol. "No one in big business should be allowed to make a faulty product and profit from it," she said.[12] Her suit was settled for an undisclosed sum.

# 8

# A LASTING LEGACY

Although a great many memorials and tributes to the *Challenger* crew were made immediately following the accident, it was three months before the crew's remains were returned to their families and final arrangements could be made. Dick Scobee and Mike Smith were both buried at Arlington National Cemetery—Mike Smith on May 3, and Dick Scobee on May 19 (his birthday). McAuliffe was buried in her hometown of Concord, New Hampshire, on April 30. Ron McNair was buried in Lake City, South Carolina, on May 17. Ellison Onizuka's remains were flown to Hawaii, where he was buried on June 7. Gregory Jarvis's remains were cremated and scattered over the Pacific Ocean near his home in Hermosa Beach, California, on May 13. Judith Resnik's remains were flown to Ohio. Her father never announced the date or place of her burial.

## The Families Carry on

Following the accident, life was difficult for the surviving families of the *Challenger* crew. Reporters camped out on their lawns. There were oceans of mail to look through and insurance matters to settle.

Slowly, the families began to cope. But most of them continued to experience delayed reactions to the tragedy. "There are still moments that my daughters break down and cry," Lorna Onizuka said in an interview with *Life* magazine in 1996, ten years after the accident.[1]

## The Legacy

Although seven brave astronauts were gone in just seventy-three seconds on that January day in 1986, they left behind a powerful legacy. Their lives would continue to impact people the world over. Perhaps the greatest impact they continue to have is on the field of education. Their families have kept this legacy alive.

The families wanted to establish a living memorial that would continue the crew's educational mission. June Scobee quit her job as an education professor at the University of Houston to found the Challenger Learning Center, an organization promoting space science for children.

"We didn't want to dwell on how the crew died, but what they had lived for," said Chuck Resnik, brother of astronaut Judith Resnik.[2] The families' goal is to establish at least one Challenger Learning Center in all fifty states and many more around the world. Their goal is quickly becoming a reality. Challenger Learning Centers have now been created across the country as well as in Canada and England, giving more than a quarter of a million students and teachers the chance to experience the excitement of space exploration.

The Challenger Learning Center in Framingham, Massachusetts, is not far from Grace Corrigan's home. She often visits the center and helps support it with the proceeds of her 1993 book, *A Journal for Christa.*

Each learning center is composed of two rooms equipped with computer hardware and software. One room is a simulated space station and the other mission control. Students and teachers work in teams to solve real-life problems during a space-flight simulation. Each mission lasts approximately forty-five minutes. Then the groups change places so that each can have an opportunity to be both on the spacecraft and in mission control. For a successful mission, each team must complete its tasks, working with its practice team. Students and teachers become involved and excited, and that excitement continues after the mission when they return to the classroom. Students become engineers and scientists as they "Rendezvous with a Comet," "Return to the Moon," "Voyage to Mars," and "Encounter Earth."[3] The faculty nation-wide for the centers includes some of the 114 Teacher in Space finalists—including McAuliffe's alternate, Barbara Morgan.

In addition to the Challenger Learning Centers, schools named after Christa McAuliffe and her fellow crew members have opened in many places. The Christa McAuliffe Planetarium was officially opened on the grounds of the New Hampshire Technical Institute in Concord, on June 21, 1990. In 1999, Grace Corrigan attended the opening of a Christa

McAuliffe school in Lima, Peru. She looks forward to the opening of even more memorials in the United States and in other countries as well. The library at Whitcomb Elementary in Clear Lake, Texas, which the Onizuka children attended, is now called the Onizuka Library.

## Status of the Teacher in Space Program

After the *Challenger* accident, many people wondered what would happen to the Teacher in Space program. For a long time, nothing happened. The program seemed to have died along with Christa McAuliffe. It was put on hold, as were plans for similar programs, including a Journalist in Space Project. NASA needed time to investigate and recover from the tragedy. Eventually, informal meetings were held on the status of the program and formal reviews of the program were held in 1993 and 1994, but no decision was reached. NASA simply stated that, should the agency decide to allow a civilian to join the shuttle crew again, the person to fill that position would be a school-teacher. Barbara Morgan, who served as Christa McAuliffe's backup, would be the Teacher in Space designee.

Over the years, Morgan has remained with the program and has always had an annual astronaut physical to keep in flight condition should the program be reinstated. Up until the fall of 1997 (when she decided to spend more time in the classroom), she traveled one week a month on education and public relations duties for the space agency.

Finally, in January 1998, Morgan got the go-ahead from NASA to begin training for a shuttle flight. She would become America's Teacher in Space and a fully trained mission specialist. NASA administrator Daniel Goldin said Morgan would be added to the astronaut roster for an unspecified flight. "I think this is great news for education," Morgan said at a January 1998 press conference.[4]

The Teacher in Space program has changed somewhat. Training is more intensive. Morgan must train for two years as part of a new class of NASA mission specialists who have education and teaching backgrounds in science, mathematics, and technology. The first year of training is general. The second year is geared to a specific shuttle mission. Morgan has already completed the first part of this training. However, it will probably be several years before she goes into space. There are many astronauts in line ahead of her.

## The Shuttle Program Today

After the *Challenger* explosion, it was more than two years before the shuttle flew again. Besides the physical changes of the aircraft itself, there was some reorganization of the space program. On October 3, 1986, an announcement was made concerning the new shuttle flight program. It was scheduled to start on February 18, 1988, with the launch of *Discovery*. Five flights were planned in 1988, ten in 1989, and eleven in 1990. The flight rate would rise to sixteen flights a year by 1994, at least half of them dedicated to space station construction and testing.

Even with all the changes and reorganization, the new shuttle program did not go as smoothly as NASA had planned. The shuttle *Discovery* did not launch according to the February 18, 1988, schedule. Instead, it launched on September 29, 1988. And although five shuttle flights were planned for 1988, only one other launch occurred that year. On December 6, 1988, the shuttle *Atlantis* left the pad for a four-day mission.

Today, the shuttle is used mainly for scientific and space station construction payloads. Though there has been no teacher in space, probably the most famous shuttle flight since the *Challenger* disaster was *Discovery* flight STS-95. This was a scientific research mission, but it also returned space pioneer John Glenn to orbit—thirty-six years, eight months, and nine days after he became the first American to orbit the earth.

The shuttle *Endeavor* was built in 1991. It would take the place of *Challenger*. The shuttle fleet would once again have four orbiters. On December 4, 1998, *Endeavor* began its twelve-day mission to assemble the International Space Station (ISS). Russian astronaut Sergei Krikalev was aboard this flight. All objectives of this mission were met. A new spacewalk record was established as astronaut Jerry L. Ross completed his seventh walk, totaling forty-four hours, nine minutes. James H. Newman moved into third place with four walks, totaling twenty-eight hours, twenty-seven minutes.

*Discovery* mission STS-96 launched on May 27, 1999. This was the first docking at the International Space Station. The United States and Russia (formerly the Soviet Union) had now come full circle after the Cold War of the early years of space exploration. Russians and Americans were now working together in space instead of competing. Perhaps what Lyndon Johnson said in 1958 will turn out to be true: "Men who have worked together to reach the stars are not likely to descend together into the depths of war and desolation."[5]

## The Future

At the time of the *Challenger* disaster, President Reagan promised, "We'll continue our quest in space. There will be more shuttle flights and more shuttle crews, and yes, more volunteers, more civilians, more teachers in space."[6] Many people thought he was being overly optimistic at the time, but now the future looks bright for the shuttle program once again. Since the shuttle resumed operation in 1988, there have been dozens of successful, safe launches and completed missions. In July 1999, Eileen Collins became the first woman shuttle commander for a mission.

What NASA administrator Daniel S. Goldin said in 1996, on the tenth anniversary of the *Challenger* accident, is still true today,

*The members of the* Challenger *crew, from left to right—Christa McAuliffe, Gregory Jarvis, Judith Resnik, Dick Scobee, Ron McNair, Mike Smith, and Ellison Onizuka. This picture of the courageous members of the* Challenger *crew was taken days before their flight. The families they left behind were determined to keep their memories alive.*

> I've said many times that safety is the highest priority at today's NASA. We will not waiver from that commitment. But human beings have always taken great risks to reap great rewards. Space flight is inherently dangerous and every member of the NASA team understands those risks.[7]

Throughout her training, McAuliffe's motto was, "Reach for the stars."[8] Through the brave men and women of NASA today, her motto lives on.

# ★ TIMELINE ★

1957—Soviet Union launches the first satellites—
*Sputnik* and *Sputnik 2*.

1958—United States successfully launches *Explorer 1*;
NASA is formed by President Dwight D.
Eisenhower.

1961—Soviet Yuri Gagarin becomes the first
human in space; Alan B. Shepard, Jr.,
becomes the first American in space.

1962—John Glenn, Jr., becomes the first American
to orbit the earth.

1963—Soviet Valentina Tereshkova becomes the
first woman in space.

1965—Soviet Alexei Leonov becomes the first
human to walk in space.

1967—*Apollo 1* catches fire during a training session
on the ground and is destroyed; All three
astronauts aboard are killed; A Soviet
cosmonaut (astronaut) dies during the
return from space.

1969—*Apollo 11* wins the space race as United
States astronauts land on the moon.

1981—The first space shuttle, *Columbia*, is
launched.

1983—Sally Ride becomes the first American
woman in space.

1984—Teacher in Space program is created.

**1985**—Christa McAuliffe is selected to become the first teacher in space.

**1986**—Space shuttle *Challenger* explodes shortly after liftoff on January 28, killing all seven crew members; President Ronald Reagan appoints a commission to investigate the cause of the explosion.

**1988**—Shuttle program resumes flights.

**1992**—Replacement orbiter, *Endeavor*, makes its first flight.

**1998**—John Glenn, Jr., returns to space aboard the shuttle *Discovery*.

**1999**—Eileen Collins becomes first woman to command the shuttle.

# ★ CHAPTER NOTES ★

## Chapter 1. Liftoff to Disaster

1. Robert T. Hohler, *I Touch the Future . . . The Story of Christa McAuliffe* (New York: Random House, 1986), p. 246.

2. *NASA, Kennedy Space Center*, n.d., <http://www.ksc.nasa.gov> (September 7, 2000).

3. Hohler, p. 248.

4. Ibid., p. 249.

5. Malcolm McConnell, *Challenger: A Major Malfunction* (Garden City, N.Y.: Doubleday & Company, Inc., 1987), p. 223.

6. Transcript of the *Challenger* Crew Comments from the Operational Recorder, NASA, Washington, D.C., 20546.

7. *National Aeronautics and Space Administration*, July 18, 2000, <http://www.hq.nasa.gov/office/pao/History/transcript.html> (September 7, 2000).

8. Claudia Glenn Dowling, "Ten Years After," *Life*, n.d., <http://www.pathfinder.com/life/space/challenger/challenger02.html> (March 19, 2000).

9. Transcript of the *Challenger* Crew Comments.

## Chapter 2. The Beginning of the Space Program

1. Alan Shepard and Deke Slayton, *Moon Shot* (Atlanta: Turner Publishing, Inc., 1994), p. 39.

2. "Soviet Satellite Sends U.S. into a Tizzy," *Life*, n.d., <http://www.lifemag.com/Life/space/giantleap/sec1/sec1.html> (September 7, 2000).

3. Shepard and Slayton, p. 42.

4. Ibid.

5. "Sputnik Forty Years Ago," *Fox News Archive*, n.d., <http://www.foxnews.com/scitech/features/sputnik> (August 1999).

6. "Soviet Satellite Sends U.S. into a Tizzy."

7. "Sputnik Forty Years Ago," *Fox News Archive.*

8. Shepard and Slayton, p. 244.

9. "Sputnik Forty Years Ago," *Fox News Archive.*

10. Grace G. Corrigan, *A Journal For Christa* (Lincoln and London: University of Nebraska Press, 1993), p. 97.

## Chapter 3. The Search for a Teacher in Space

1. Grace G. Corrigan, *A Journal for Christa* (Lincoln and London: University of Nebraska Press, 1993), p. 85.

2. Liz Matson, "The Century Project: Christa McAuliffe—Challenger Space Shuttle Explosion," n.d., <http://www.bostonherald.com/bostonherald/Ionw/centurymcauliffe10271999.htm> (March 14, 2000).

3. Robert T. Hohler, *I Touch the Future . . . The Story of Christa McAuliffe* (New York: Random House, 1986), p. 71.

4. Ibid., p. 76.

5. Corrigan, p. 98.

6. Ibid., p. 100.

7. Ibid., p. 94.

## Chapter 4. The *Challenger* Crew Prepares

1. Robert T. Hohler, *I Touch the Future . . . The Story of Christa McAuliffe* (New York: Random House, 1986), p. 154.

2. Ibid., p. 150.

3. "Judith Resnik," *The Jewish Student Online Research Center (JSource)*, 2000, <http://www.us-israel.org/jsource/biography/Resnik.html> (September 7, 2000).

4. Malcolm McConnell, *Challenger: A Major Malfunction* (Garden City, N.Y.: Doubleday & Company, Inc., 1987), p. 97.

5. William Harwood, "Chapter One: The Mission 1986," *Voyage Into History*, n.d., <http://cbsnews.cbs.com/network/news/space/51Lchap1mission.html>, (October 13, 2000.)

6. McConnell, p. 258.

7. "Statement of Senator Daniel K. Akaka Dedication of Solar-Powered Pathfinder World Record Flight to the Memory of Colonel Ellison S. Onizuka and the Children of Hawaii," *Daniel K. Akaka, Hawaii's Senator*, n.d., <http://www.senate.gov/~akaka/speeches/971210.html> (September 7, 2000).

8. Ibid.

9. *Christa McAuliffe Bio.*, n.d., <http://www.starhop.com/cm_bio.html> (September 7, 2000).

## Chapter 5. Preparing for Launch

1. Report of the Presidential Commission on the Space Shuttle *Challenger* Accident, Washington, D.C., 1986, p. 161.

2. Ibid., pp. 249–250.

3. Malcolm McConnell, *Challenger: A Major Malfunction* (Garden City, N.Y.: Doubleday & Company, Inc., 1987), p. 22.

4. John Gillespie Magee, Jr., *High Flight*, n.d., <http://www.cs.unlv.edu/-rho/interests/other/poems/magee/flight.html> (September 7, 2000).

## Chapter 6. After the Tragedy

1. Malcolm McConnell, *Challenger: A Major Malfunction* (Garden City, N.Y.: Doubleday & Company, Inc., 1987), p. 247.

2. Richard S. Lewis, *Challenger: The Final Voyage* (New York: Columbia University Press, 1988), p. 25.

3. "President Reagan's Speech on The Challenger Disaster," *The Ronald Reagan Home Page*, 1994–1999, <http://reagan.webteamone.com/speeches/challenger.html> (September 7, 2000).

4. "Reagan's Remarks," *Houston Chronicle.com*, n.d., <http://www.chron.com/content/interactive/special/challenger/docs/reagan.html> (March 19, 2000).

5. "A President's Eulogy," *Houston Chronicle.com*, n.d., <http://www.chron.com/content/interactive/special/challenger/docs/eulogy/html> (March 19, 2000).

6. Grace G. Corrigan, *A Journal for Christa* (Lincoln and London: University of Nebraska Press, 1993), p. 136.

## Chapter 7. The Investigation

1. "Preface—Report of the Presidential Commission on the Space Shuttle *Challenger* Accident," Kennedy Space Center—NASA, January 27, 1996, <http://science.ksc.nasa.gov/shuttle/missions/51-l/docs/rogers-commission/Preface.txt> (September 7, 2000).

2. Kennedy Space Center—NASA, <http://science.ksc.nasa.gov/shuttle/missions/51-l/docs/rogers-commission/commission.txt> (October 13, 2000).

3. Report of the Presidential Commission on the Space Shuttle Challenger Accident, Washington, D.C., 1986, p. 148.

4. Claudia Glenn Dowling, <http://www.pathfinder.com/Life/space/challenger/challenger05.html>.

5. "From Disaster to Discovery," Great TV News Stories, ABC News Video (1989).

6. "Joseph P. Kerwin to Richard H. Truly, July 28, 1986," *National Aeronautics and Space Administration*, January 24, 1996, <http://www.hq.nasa.gov/office/pao/History/kerwin.html> (March 19, 2000).

7. Report of the Presidential Commission, p. 1.

8. Ibid., p. 4.

9. "Recommendations of the Presidential Commission," *Kennedy Space Center—NASA*, n.d., <http://science.ksc.nasa.gov/shuttle/missions/51-l/docs/rogers-commission/table-of-contents.html> (September 7, 2000).

10. Ibid.

11. Richard S. Lewis, *Challenger: The Final Voyage* (New York: Columbia University Press, 1988), p. 223.

12. Dowling, <http://www.pathfinder.com/Life/space/challenger/challenger05.html>.

## Chapter 8. A Lasting Legacy

1. Claudia Glenn Dowling, <http://www.pathfinder. com/Life/space/challenger/challenger06.html>.

2. Ibid.

3. "Challenger Learning Center Scenarios," *Challenger Center Online*, n.d., <http://www.challenger.org/clc/ clc_scen_set.htm> (March 19, 2000).

4. "Teacher-in-Space Morgan Scheduled to Begin Astronaut Training," *SpaceViews, The Online Publication of Space Exploration*, n.d., <http://www.spaceviews.com/ 1998/02/01b.html> (March 19, 2000).

5. "U.S. Senator Lyndon Baines Johnson, Addressing the U.N. General Assembly, 1958," *National Aeronautics and Space Administration*, December 23, 1999, <http:// spaceflight.nasa.gov/history/shuttle-mir> (March 19, 2000).

6. Dowling, <http://www.pathfinder.com/Life/space/ challenger/challenger04.html>.

7. "NASA Administrator on Tenth Anniversary of Challenger Accident," *National Aeronautics and Space Administration*, January 24, 1996, <http://www.hq.nasa. gov/office/pao/History/administrator.html> (March 19, 2000).

8. Robert T. Hohler, *I Touch the Future . . . The Story of Christa McAuliffe* (New York: Random House, 1986), p. 182.

# ★ FURTHER READING ★

Biel, Timothy Levi. *The Challenger*. San Diego, Calif.: Lucent Books, 1990.

Corrigan, Grace G. *A Journal for Christa*. Lincoln and London: University of Nebraska Press, 1993.

Lewis, Richard S. *Challenger: The Final Voyage*. New York: Columbia University Press, 1988.

McConnell, Malcolm. *Challenger: A Major Malfunction*. Garden City, N.Y.: Doubleday & Company, Inc., 1987.

# ★ INTERNET ADDRESSES ★

Challenger Center Online. n.d., <http://www.challenger.org/> (September 7, 2000).

*National Aeronautics and Space Administration*. July 18, 2000. <http://www.hq.nasa.gov/office/pao/History/transcript.html> (September 7, 2000).

"Report of the Presidential Commission on the Space Shuttle *Challenger* Accident." *Kennedy Space Center—NASA*. January 27, 1996. <http://science.ksc.nasa.gov/shuttle/missions/51-l/docs/rogers-commission/table-of-contents.html> (September 7, 2000).

# ★ INDEX ★